The Final Battle for Earth

The Final Battle for Earth

Unlocking the Mysteries of the Coming Great
Tribulation and Wrath of God

OBINNA C. D. ANEJIONU

RESOURCE *Publications* • Eugene, Oregon

THE FINAL BATTLE FOR EARTH
Unlocking the Mysteries of the Coming Great Tribulation and Wrath of God

Copyright © 2022 Obinna C. D. Anejionu. All rights reserved. Except for brief quotations in critical publications or reviews, no part of this book may be reproduced in any manner without prior written permission from the publisher. Write: Permissions, Wipf and Stock Publishers, 199 W. 8th Ave., Suite 3, Eugene, OR 97401.

Resource Publications
An Imprint of Wipf and Stock Publishers
199 W. 8th Ave., Suite 3
Eugene, OR 97401

www.wipfandstock.com

PAPERBACK ISBN: 978-1-6667-4812-3
HARDCOVER ISBN: 978-1-6667-4813-0
EBOOK ISBN: 978-1-6667-4814-7

08/15/22

Italics have been added to Scripture quotations.

Unless otherwise indicated, Scripture quotations are from the ESV® Bible (The Holy Bible, English Standard Version®), copyright © 2001 by Crossway, a publishing ministry of Good News Publishers. Used by permission. All rights reserved.

Scripture quotations marked AV are from the Authorized (King James) Version and are reproduced by permission of the United Kingdom Crown's patentee, Cambridge University Press.

Scripture quotations marked CEV are from the Contemporary English Version, copyright © 1991, 1992, 1995 by the American Bible Society. Used by permission.

Scripture quotations marked CPDV are from the Catholic Public Domain Version Bible.

Scripture quotations marked LB are from the Living Bible, copyright © 1971. Used by permission of Tyndale House Publishers. All rights reserved.

Scriptures quotations marked NIV are from the Holy Bible, New International Version®, copyright © 1973, 1978, 1984, 2011 by Biblica, Inc.™ Used by permission of Zondervan. All rights reserved worldwide.

Scripture quotations marked NKJV are from the New King James Version, copyright © 1982 by Thomas Nelson, Inc. Used by permission. All rights reserved.

Scripture quotations marked NLT are from the Holy Bible, New Living Translation, copyright © 1996, 2004, 2015 by Tyndale House Foundation. Used by permission of Tyndale House Publishers. All rights reserved.

Scripture quotations marked Weymouth NT are from the Weymouth New Testament, public domain.

Scripture quotations marked RSV Catholic ed. are from the Revised Standard Version of the Bible: Catholic Edition, copyright @ 1965, 1966, the Division of Christian Education of the National Council of the Churches of Christ in the United States of America. Used by permission. All rights reserved.

Scripture quotations marked YLT are from Young's Literal Translation (1898) by Robert Young.

To my wife and children

Contents

Preface: Unravelling Key Revelation Puzzles		ix
Acknowledgment		xiii
1	Introduction	1
2	Letters to the Seven Churches	17
3	The Precursors: Emergence of the Four Horsemen	36
4	The Great Tribulation	68
5	The Seventh Seal: The Wrath of God	99
6	The Seventh Trumpet: The Last Trump	121
7	Exegesis	156
Bibliography		175

Preface:
Unravelling Key Revelation Puzzles

The book of Revelation is an intriguing and important book to every Christian. As the lynchpin of biblical eschatology, the book contains key information on various events that will take place on earth before the return of Jesus Christ. However, the deep mysteries that it contains either frighten or confound many Christians. Many Christians are afraid to dabble in it. Those who dare to get into it are usually confused by the intricate and convoluted mysteries it contains. The book of Revelation is a prophetic jigsaw puzzle that contains all the pieces of the end-time and requires careful arrangement of the pieces, for the hidden meanings to crystalize.

Some of the issues many Christians face with understanding the book of Revelation include:

- Bad reading/interpretation of Scripture
- Misunderstanding of the sequence of events
- Misinterpretation of signs, symbols, and figures of speech used in the book

Hence, this book is an attempt to clear the air around some of these and make the book of Revelation clearer for readers to understand.

The motivation for writing this book mostly stemmed from my quest to gain a better understanding of the events of the end-time. Like many others, I had initially relied on the interpretations and teachings of renowned and respected Bible scholars and preachers to bring clearer understanding to this. However, the conflicting postulations and interpretations of these end-time events by various Bible scholars and preachers are bringing more confusion than clarity. Currently, eschatology is a topical issue, and the book of Revelation is a highly discussed book among Christians. The internet, social media, and YouTube are rife with various teachings, interpretations, theories, and end-time prophecies. Unfortunately, rather than elucidating the issue, many of these arguments add to the complexity of the book of Revelation. It became imperative that an objective approach, devoid of any doctrinal bias, and a fresh pair of eyes, unencumbered with an entrenched end-time position, is required to clearly interpret the events and symbolisms revealed in the book of Revelation. Hence, this prompted me to reanalyze the book of Revelation by deploying scientific analytical methods to decipher the hidden meanings in the events described in the book. The primary intent was to help myself and others with a similar quest to understand these events.

By analyzing the nuances contained in the several visions presented in the book of Revelation and review of other relevant Scriptures in the Bible, this book brings out several salient points that may have been missed by previous scholars. The key purpose of this book was to make it easier for people to understand the chronology of events of Revelation and to have a greater grasp of the contents, to fully prepare for the coming events that will shake the foundations of the world.

This book explores new insights that may have been missed by previous eschatological scholars and calls for discourse within the Christian community. This is not to say that I have covered everything, and there may be some areas in which I may have had blinders in my interpretation of the meanings of the signs and symbols used in the book of Revelation ("For we know in part and we prophesy in part" [1 Cor 13:9–10]). There are many symbols and signs used in the book of Revelation with multiple meanings that may not be clearly understood until the end days. This piece is just my contribution to the existing body of knowledge in this regard. It is left for readers to individually reassess my interpretations and ask the Holy Spirit of God to reveal the truth to them. To this end, for every topic I have used in this book, I have left the exact quotes from the Bible, to enable people to easily cross-reference. It is the duty of every man to seek the truth for himself. Remember Jesus Christ's warning ("See that no one leads you astray" [Matt 24:4]).

In conclusion, this book was written to:

- unravel the mysteries of the book of Revelation
- enable Christians and the rest of humanity to understand the implications of unfolding world events and how they relate to eschatology
- get Christians ready for what is about to come upon the world
- enable Christians to clearly understand what God expects us to do during the coming times

- preach the gospel of Jesus to the world, and
- encourage objective and more vibrant discourse of the mysteries of the book of Revelation, unhinged from long-held opinions, views, and doctrines of the end-times

Inasmuch as I have done my best to present the truth as far as God permitted and as the Spirit led me to understand, do not solely rely on my interpretation or consider the information in this book as doctrinal truth. Do your own research, and always cross-check all information with the Bible. This book is intended to stimulate people to reexamine the facts from an unclouded and objective perspective, unencumbered by previous dogmatic and doctrinal proclivities. Importantly, consult the Holy Spirit to guide and enlighten you in this regard.

It is expected that this book will enable readers to have a better understanding of the contents of the book of Revelation, ginger Christians to reanalyze previously held opinions as well as provoke robust, biblically sound, and fact-based end-time discussions among Christians, in order to build up further knowledge and insights on the coming period of great distress in the world.

Acknowledgment

I wish to extend my special thanks to Sir Percy L. Ahiarammunnah for making time to review the early drafts of this book.

1

Introduction

1.1. IN THE BEGINNING

The coming events relayed in the book of Revelation are not random events, but rather a well-thought-out plan to take over the world from Satan and hand it back to God. The events are in a real sense a culmination of those that started from Genesis, when God's original plan for man was disrupted by events orchestrated by the fall of Adam. The story could be summarized thus: God handed the earth over to Adam to take charge of. Adam lost this mandate/authority after the fall, when Satan deceived him and Eve. Hence, Satan surreptitiously usurped the authority of Adam to become the ruler of the world. Satan reminded Jesus that he has authority over the earth while tempting him, and Christ did not refute this claim:

> Then the devil, taking Him up on a high mountain, showed Him all the kingdoms of the world in a moment of time. [6] And the devil said to Him, "All this authority I will give You, and their glory; for this has been delivered to me, and I give it to whomever I wish. [7] Therefore, if You will worship before me, all will be Yours." (Luke 4:5–7 NKJV)

Christ also referred to this ruler of the earth in John 16:

> And when He has come, He will convict the world of sin, and of righteousness, and of judgment: [9] of sin, because they do not believe in Me; [10] of righteousness, because I go to My Father

and you see Me no more; [11] *of judgment, because the ruler of this world is judged* (John 16:8–11 NKJV)

Also, St. Paul wrote:

> Satan, who is the god of this world, has blinded the minds of those who don't believe. They are unable to see the glorious light of the Good News. They don't understand this message about the glory of Christ, who is the exact likeness of God. (2 Cor 4:4)

Jesus Christ paved the way for the legitimate reclamation of this authority from Satan by his death on the cross and eventual resurrection. Since Satan took the kingship of the earth from a man (Adam), through sin, only a man can legally reclaim this kingship, by overcoming the power of sin. However, no man prior to the coming of Jesus was able to achieve this feat of raising man from his fallen state. Therefore, to salvage humanity from its fallen position, and bring it back to its rightful place originally ordained by God, Jesus Christ had to come as a man to overcome the power of sin and open the gateway for the redemption of man. In other words, God had to come as a man to defeat Satan. Jesus was very emphatic in referring to himself as the Son of Man, because only a man can legally defeat Satan and reclaim the authority. Jesus hinted at the purpose of his mission when he declared thus:

> "Now is my soul troubled. And what shall I say? 'Father, save me from this hour'? But for this purpose I have come to this hour. [28] Father, glorify your name." Then a voice came from heaven: "I have glorified it, and I will glorify it again." [29] The crowd that stood there and heard it said that it had thundered. Others said, "An angel has spoken to him." [30] Jesus answered, "This voice has come for your sake, not mine. [31] Now is the judgment of this world; now will the ruler of this world be cast out. [32] And I, when I am lifted up from the earth, will draw all people to myself." (John 12:27–32)

This reclamation of the authority from Satan was reechoed by St. Paul in his First Letter to the Corinthians. He hinted that the death of Christ on the cross and his resurrection was essentially a coup d'état to dethrone Satan from being the ruler of this word. This is the reason the essence of this project (Project Jesus Christ) was kept as a highly classified secret until it was fully accomplished:

> But we impart a secret and hidden wisdom of God, which God decreed before the ages for our glory. [8] None of the rulers of this

age understood this, for if they had, they would not have crucified the Lord of glory. (1 Cor 2:7–8)

This was reiterated in Revelation, that Christ redeemed humanity from every tribe for God:

> You are worthy to take the scroll and to open its seals, because you were slain, and with your blood you purchased for God persons from every tribe and language and people and nation.[10] You have made them to be a kingdom and priests to serve our God, and they will reign on the earth. (Rev 5:9–10)

Hence, Christ's salvation extended beyond the Jews. People from every tribe, language, and nation were rescued for the kingdom of God.

Despite having legally lost his authority over the earth, Satan, who neither plays fair nor according to the rules, is still holding on to power and his influence on the affairs of men. Thus, he must be crushed and imprisoned for all his atrocities. The purpose of the second coming of Jesus is to complete the job of wresting power from Satan and establishing the kingdom of God on earth. This final battle to crush Satan and his minions and wrest power from him (events contained in the book of Revelation) will be accomplished during the end of age. This will be accompanied by a series of cataclysmic natural and anthropogenic events (hunger, economic crisis, war, pandemics) and unprecedented natural disasters (most of which may be attributed to climate change) that will be experienced by humanity in the last days. These events will be increasing in both frequency and intensity as God wraps up the agenda to reclaim the world from Satan. At the fringe of the last days, Satan will be allowed a brief period to reign on earth before he is defeated by the armies of heaven, and Christ will regain control of the earth and set up the kingdom of God on earth for a thousand years.

Hence, the declaration at the blowing of the seventh trumpet:

> Then the seventh angel blew his trumpet, and there were loud voices in heaven, saying, "The kingdom of the world has become the kingdom of our Lord and of his Christ, and he shall reign forever and ever." (Rev 11:15)

This initial one thousand-year period of the reign of Christ on earth is commonly referred as the millennial reign of Christ. After this, Satan will be released from prison for a short time to face Jesus Christ yet again in a final battle, where he will be ultimately defeated and finally sent to the lake of fire. This will mark the end of the present earth. A new earth and new heaven will be created as a new cycle commences.

Satan knows about this, and his key strategy is either to delay this or take as many people as possible to hell. He wants to deprive them of the bliss of eternal life with God, as has been promised.

1.2. AUTHENTIC AND UPDATED REVELATION OF JESUS CHRIST

The revelation of Jesus Christ, which God gave him to show to his servants the things that must soon take place. He made it known by sending his angel to his servant John, [2] who bore witness to the word of God and to the testimony of Jesus Christ, even to all that he saw. [3] Blessed is the one who reads aloud the words of this prophecy, and blessed are those who hear, and who keep what is written in it, for the time is near.

[4] John to the seven churches that are in Asia:

Grace to you and peace from him who is and who was and who is to come, and from the seven spirits who are before his throne, [5] and from Jesus Christ the faithful witness, the firstborn of the dead, and the ruler of kings on earth.

To him who loves us and has freed us from our sins by his blood [6] and made us a kingdom, priests to his God and Father, to him be glory and dominion forever and ever. Amen. [7] Behold, he is coming with the clouds, and every eye will see him, even those who pierced him, and all tribes of the earth will wail on account of him. Even so. Amen.

[8] "I am the Alpha and the Omega," says the Lord God, "who is and who was and who is to come, the Almighty."

[9] I, John, your brother and partner in the tribulation and the kingdom and the patient endurance that are in Jesus, was on the island called Patmos on account of the word of God and the testimony of Jesus. [10] I was in the Spirit on the Lord's day, and I heard behind me a loud voice like a trumpet [11] saying, "Write what you see in a book and send it to the seven churches, to Ephesus and to Smyrna and to Pergamum and to Thyatira and to Sardis and to Philadelphia and to Laodicea."

[12] Then I turned to see the voice that was speaking to me, and on turning I saw seven golden lampstands, [13] and in the midst of the lampstands one like a son of man, clothed with a long robe and with a golden sash around his chest. [14] The hairs of his head were white, like white wool, like snow. His eyes were like a flame of fire, [15] his feet were like burnished bronze, refined in a furnace, and his voice was like the roar of many waters. [16] In his right hand

INTRODUCTION 5

he held seven stars, from his mouth came a sharp two-edged sword, and his face was like the sun shining in full strength. [17] When I saw him, I fell at his feet as though dead. But he laid his right hand on me, saying, "Fear not, I am the first and the last, [18] and the living one. I died, and behold I am alive forevermore, and I have the keys of Death and Hades. [19] Write therefore the things that you have seen, those that are and those that are to take place after this. [20] As for the mystery of the seven stars that you saw in my right hand, and the seven golden lampstands, the seven stars are the angels of the seven churches, and the seven lampstands are the seven churches. (Rev 1:9–20)

The book of Revelation starts with an elaborate description of St. John's encounter with Jesus Christ. At the point of encounter, John is on the island of Patmos where he has been exiled. This revelation of events that will happen during the last days is given to John by Jesus Christ. It adds extra details to previous insights of end-time events he had given to his disciples while on earth and to those in ancient prophecies of Daniel and other prophets who had hinted at the things that would happen towards the time of the return of Jesus Christ. Hence, for believers, this account of end-time events is authentic, true, and trustworthy and supersedes any other eschatological prophecy previously recorded in the Bible. For the yet to be converted to the Christian faith, they are also encouraged to read this book with an open mind, assessing the revelations and interpretations based on the merits of the facts presented.

1.3. THE REVELATION OF FUTURE AND NOT PAST EVENTS

The revelation of Jesus Christ, which God gave him to show to his servants the things that must soon take place. He made it known by sending his angel to his servant John, [2] who bore witness to the word of God and to the testimony of Jesus Christ, even to all that he saw. [3] Blessed is the one who reads aloud the words of this prophecy, and blessed are those who hear, and who keep what is written in it, for the time is near. (Rev 1:1–4)

The first verse of the book of Revelation clearly sets the mind of the reader to the fact that what is going to be revealed are things that must happen in the future ("that must soon take place") and not what has occurred in the past:

Write, therefore, what you have seen, what is now and what will take place later. (Rev 1:20)

John was clearly instructed to write about what is present and will soon take place and not *what has happened in the past.* It is vitally important to note this fact, as there are some aspects of the visions in the book of Revelation that seem to present a recap of past things. It is obvious that God decided to make this clear from the outset, so that readers would properly be guided on how to read and understand the words being revealed.

Admittedly, the manner through which the facts were revealed in the book of Revelation is a bit convoluted, so that many readers tend to be confounded with the core message being revealed. Many prominent Christian preachers and Bible scholars have concluded that some aspects of the book are flashbacks of things that had happened in the past. Many doctrines have been built on this erroneous assumption. This is essentially due to the inability to link the sequence of events revealed in the book in the correct order. This logic of reading the book as a vision of past, present, and future things adds more confusion, which makes people miss the core message. Another point to note is that past events, such as events surrounding the birth of Jesus Christ, cannot in a true sense be revealed after the fact, as people who had experienced those events already would have known about it. We cannot really pass off what happened in the past as a revelation. Hence, God could not have told us he was revealing things that "must happen soon," only to loop back and show us things that had happened previously.

The events in Revelation were unfolding as the seven seals were being opened by the Lamb that was slain:

> Then I saw in the right hand of him who was seated on the throne a scroll written within and on the back, sealed with seven seals. [2] And I saw a mighty angel proclaiming with a loud voice, "Who is worthy to open the scroll and break its seals?" [3] And no one in heaven or on earth or under the earth was able to open the scroll or to look into it, [4] and I began to weep loudly because no one was found worthy to open the scroll or to look into it. [5] And one of the elders said to me, "Weep no more; behold, the Lion of the tribe of Judah, the Root of David, has conquered, so that he can open the scroll and its seven seals."
>
> [6] And between the throne and the four living creatures and among the elders I saw a Lamb standing, as though it had been slain, with seven horns and with seven eyes, which are the seven spirits of God sent out into all the earth. [7] And he went and took the scroll from the right hand of him who was seated on the throne. (Rev 5:1–7)

Take note that prior to the time this heavenly assembly was convened, no one was able to open the sealed scroll. Hence, there is no chance that

INTRODUCTION

these events would have happened. The fact that the seals were opened by Jesus Christ after he had been crucified buttresses the point that the events were planned to happen after Christ has been crucified. This will become clearer as we go further in the book of Revelation.

1.4. THE RULE OF SEVENS—COMPLETION OF GOD'S AGENDA FOR EARTH

It seems God prepared the events of the last days using a spiritual code based on the rule of seven. In ancient Israelite culture, the number seven communicated a sense of completeness or fullness.[1] The number seven was copiously used in the visions contained in the book of Revelation. The events presented in the book of Revelation are broken into stages: seven letters, seven seals, seven trumpets, and seven bowls. Each of these marks distinct key periods connected to the end-time, with events in each stage directly flowing into the next until the culmination.

- The letters to the seven churches mark the period Christians will be making final preparations for the events of the end-time and return of Jesus Christ.
- The opening of the seven seals covers the period Satan and his minions will be permitted to physically infiltrate and briefly take over the world. It covers the precursor period (pretribulation/beginning of persecution) and the great tribulation period, when Satan, the antichrist, and the fallen ones will unleash unprecedented wickedness on humanity.
- The seven-trumpets period covers the time when God's judgment of earth and its inhabitants commences.
- The seven-bowl period covers the time when the final wrath of God is unleashed.

In addition to the seven sequences used to mark the various events of the last days, there are other places the number seven was used. For example:

- In his right hand he held seven stars. (Rev 1:12–16)
- The seven stars are the angels of the seven churches. (Rev 1:20)
- I saw seven golden lampstands, and in the midst of the lampstands one like a son of man. (Rev 1:12–13)
- The seven lampstands are the seven churches. (Rev 1:20)

1. Mackie, "Significance of Seven."

- In front of the throne, seven lamps were blazing. These are the seven spirits of God. (Rev 4:6)
- The Lamb had seven horns and seven eyes, which are the seven spirits of God sent out into all the earth. (Rev 5:6).

Although the full meaning of the use of seven in this book may not be immediately clear to readers or fully grasped, it is still worth noting that something is really going on with the number seven, with respect to the events contained in the book of Revelation. Perhaps God is trying to tell humanity that the events of revelation will bring to completion his agenda for earth. This is made evident towards the end of the Revelation, when a new heaven and earth appeared, as the previous earth and heaven have passed away (completed their cycle):

"Then I saw "a new heaven and a new earth," for the first heaven and the first earth had passed away, and there was no longer any sea." (Rev 21:1 NIV).

1.5. EXPATIATION OF MATT 24, LUKE 21, AND MARK 13

The events described in Rev 6 are expatiation of the events of the last days ("sign of your coming and of the end of the age" [Matt 24:3 NIV]) described by Jesus Christ as recorded in the Gospels (Matt 24, Luke 21, and Mark 13). In the account recorded in the Gospels, Jesus Christ succinctly presented the highlights of the events. However, the sequence of events outlined in the Gospel accounts throws light on how the events in the book of Revelation should be interpreted. Therefore, relevant texts in the Gospels are used in this book to enhance the understanding of the visions in the book of Revelation and ensure the consistency of the interpretations thereof. Insights are also drawn from relevant Old Testament books, especially from the books of the prophets where key aspects of the end-time are revealed. Hence, as we continue this study, pointers will be made to other parts of the Scripture where those events have been hinted at.

1.6. SEQUENCE OF END-TIME EVENTS

Strictly speaking, the visions in the book of Revelation are not presented in chronological or sequential order. Although there is a semblance of chronology/sequence in certain aspects/chapters, visions from different stages of the events are inserted into previous or future stages of the end-time. Also, some events appear to be happening simultaneously, even though they are recorded in the book as if they occur in sequence. This style of presentation is what mostly throws off many readers of the book. It seems God intentionally juggled the events in order not to prematurely give out the secrets in the visions to casual readers. However, a diligent and careful interpretation of the chapters will reveal the underlying sequence of the key events of the last days contained in the book. As if to complicate matters, the key stages are presented in a nested sequence pattern (sequence within sequence). For example, the events of the seventh seal consist of seven separate events (the seven trumpets). Likewise, the seventh trumpet contains the seven bowls of God's wrath. Table 1.1 summarizes the sequence of key events hinged on the cardinal sequence of events (i.e., the seven seals).

Table 1.1. *Sequence of key end-time events*

Seal 1	Seal 2	Seal 3	Seal 4	Seal 5	Seal 6	Seal 7
Precursor events/birth pains				Increasing persecution of Christians	Fall of Satan, rebellious principalities, and heavenly powers to earth (from the second heaven)	Wrath of God and Christ (seven trumpets)
						Seven bowls
					The church goes into the wilderness	Christ returns to earth
					Great tribulation	Battle of Armageddon and defeat of Satan
					Great multitudes found in heaven	First resurrection
						Millennial reign
						Final war
					Celestial preparation for the coming of Christ and judgment of the world	White throne judgment

1.7. WHAT DOES GOD EXPECT FROM CHRISTIANS DURING THE GREAT TRIBULATION?

Despite the predilections of many Christians for various end-time theories concerning the great tribulation (pre-, mid-, and post-tribulation rapture), hinged essentially on the belief that God will extract Christians from the earth to heaven, to preserve them from the calamitous events of the end-time, God actually expects Christians to be on earth as courageous bearers/witnesses of the gospel during this critical period—to carry on with the gospel of Jesus and present testimonies to unbelievers. During the precursor period God expects that the testimonies of Christ should be intensified across the world so that more souls can be saved:

> But before all this they will lay *their hands on you and persecute you*, delivering you up to the synagogues and prisons, and you will be brought before kings and governors for my name's sake. [13] *This will be your opportunity to bear witness.* (Luke 21:12-13)

Only Christians on earth will be able to carry out this task, not those in heaven. If Christians are removed from the earth before the great tribulation, who would carry out this important end-time task?

However, at the beginning of the great tribulation, Jesus Christ expects believers to flee to safe places and especially avoid Jerusalem, as that would be the epicentre of the devastating action of the antichrist:

So when you see the abomination of desolation spoken of by the prophet Daniel, standing in the holy place (let the reader understand), [16] then let those who are in Judea flee to the mountains. [17] Let the one who is on the housetop not go down to take what is in his house, [18] and let the one who is in the field not turn back to take his cloak. (Matt 24:15-18)

Based on various information in the book of Revelation; the Gospel accounts of the end-time period in Matthew, Mark, and Luke; and the book of Daniel, there is really no mention of a rapture event that will lead to Christians suddenly being taken to heaven from earth—similar to the Ascension of Jesus Christ.

The reality is that many Christians will be killed during this period and their souls received in heaven:

> When he opened the fifth seal, I saw under the altar the souls of those who had been slain for the word of God and for the witness they had borne. [10] They cried out with a loud voice, "O Sovereign Lord, holy and true, how long before you will judge and avenge our blood on those who dwell on the earth?" [11] Then they were each given a white robe and told to rest a little longer, until the

number of their fellow servants and their brothers should be complete, who were to be killed as they themselves had been. (Rev 6:9–11)

This is also made abundantly clear in Rev 7, when the souls of multitudes from every nation were found in heaven and were described as those who came out from the great tribulation:

> [9] After this I looked, and behold, a great multitude that no one could number, from every nation, from all tribes and peoples and languages, standing before the throne and before the Lamb, clothed in white robes, with palm branches in their hands, [10] and crying out with a loud voice, "Salvation belongs to our God who sits on the throne, and to the Lamb!" [11] And all the angels were standing around the throne and around the elders and the four living creatures, and they fell on their faces before the throne and worshiped God, [12] saying, "Amen! Blessing and glory and wisdom and thanksgiving and honor and power and might be to our God forever and ever! Amen."
>
> [13] Then one of the elders addressed me, saying, "Who are these, clothed in white robes, and from where have they come?" [14] I said to him, "Sir, you know." And he said to me, "These are the ones coming out of the great tribulation. They have washed their robes and made them white in the blood of the Lamb.
>
> [15] "Therefore they are before the throne of God, and serve him day and night in his temple; and he who sits on the throne will shelter them with his presence. [16] They shall hunger no more, neither thirst anymore; the sun shall not strike them, nor any scorching heat. [17] For the Lamb in the midst of the throne will be their shepherd, and he will guide them to springs of living water, and God will wipe away every tear from their eyes." (Rev 7:9–17)

To buttress this point, Jesus made it very clear that Christians will face the great tribulation. This was the reason he took time in the Gospels to explain the details of things to watch out for and encouraged his followers to endure to the end:

> "See that no one leads you astray. [5] For many will come in my name, saying, 'I am the Christ,' and they will lead many astray. [6] And you will hear of wars and rumours of wars. See that you are not alarmed, for this must take place, but the end is not yet. [7] For nation will rise against nation, and kingdom against kingdom,

and there will be famines and earthquakes in various places. ⁸ All these are but the beginning of the birth pains.

⁹ *"Then they will deliver you up to tribulation and put you to death, and you will be hated by all nations for my name's sake.* ¹⁰ And then many will fall away and betray one another and hate one another. ¹¹ And many false prophets will arise and lead many astray. ¹² And because lawlessness will be increased, the love of many will grow cold. ¹³ But the one who endures to the end will be saved. ¹⁴ And this gospel of the kingdom will be proclaimed throughout the whole world as a testimony to all nations, and then the end will come. (Matt 24:4–14)

Daniel also hinted at this:

And the wise among the people shall make many understand, though for some days they shall stumble by sword and flame, by captivity and plunder. ³⁴ When they stumble, they shall receive a little help. And many shall join themselves to them with flattery, ³⁵ and some of the wise shall stumble, so that they may be refined, purified, and made white, until the time of the end, for it still awaits the appointed time. (Dan 11:33–35)

The danger in believing and preparing for a rapture that would take some or all Christians out of this world before the antichrist begins his persecution of the world is that many Christians would be disappointed and at a loss on how to handle the persecution. Hence, instead of preparing for how to spread the gospel and testimonies of Christ during this period, Christians are complacent and relying on the rapture as an escape plan. An ill-prepared Christian would be highly inefficient in bearing the good news of Christ to an unbelieving world. On the contrary, preparing to face the great tribulation will not do Christians any harm if somehow God decides to extract Christians before it commences. Preparing for war that eventually does not happen is better than not preparing for a war that happens.

However, there are indications that some Christians will be preserved from the great tribulation (wrath of Satan). Based on interpretation of the mystery of the woman and the dragon, there is a high likelihood that certain Christians will be hidden somewhere on earth called the wilderness, where they will wait for three and a half years (1,260 days) until Christ returns to earth. Compared to the rapture, the going-into-the-wilderness event is a horizontal action that will result in some people living in a hidden part of the earth where Satan and antichrist will be unable to get to them:

And a great sign appeared in heaven: a woman clothed with the sun, with the moon under her feet, and on her head a crown of twelve stars. ² She was pregnant and was crying out in birth pains and the agony of giving birth. ³ And another sign appeared in heaven: behold, a great red dragon, with seven heads and ten horns, and on his heads seven diadems. ⁴ His tail swept down a third of the stars of heaven and cast them to the earth. And the dragon stood before the woman who was about to give birth, so that when she bore her child he might devour it. ⁵ She gave birth to a male child, one who is to rule all the nations with a rod of iron, but her child was caught up to God and to his throne, ⁶ and the woman fled into the wilderness, where she has a place prepared by God, in which she is to be nourished for 1,260 days. (Rev 12:1–6)

There is an indication that this set of Christians will be those whose lifestyles match those of the church of Philadelphia:

Because you have kept my word about patient endurance, I will keep you from the hour of trial that is coming on the whole world, to try those who dwell on the earth. ¹¹ I am coming soon. Hold fast what you have, so that no one may seize your crown. (Rev 3:10)

1.8. TRIBULATION VERSUS WRATH

One of the keys to understanding the book of Revelation is the ability to clearly distinguish the tribulation from the wrath of God. The tribulation period is a period that God permits Satan and his cohorts to exercise their power on earth to the fullest. This period covers the events of the first seal to end of the sixth seal. Hence, it is a period when Satan through the antichrist, fallen angels, and human agents will unleash his wrath on anyone opposing his authority or refusing to worship him as God—mainly, Christians and Jews. However, the wrath is the period when God will punish/judge the world, Satan, and all his followers on earth for their wickedness against the children of God. The period of God's wrath is contained within the seventh seal. Hence, towards the end of the events of the sixth seal, the kings of the earth declare that the time of God's wrath has come:

Then the kings of the earth and the great ones and the generals and the rich and the powerful, and everyone, slave and free, hid themselves in the caves and among the rocks of the mountains, ¹⁶ calling to the mountains and rocks, "Fall on us and hide us from the face of him who is seated on the throne, and from

> *the wrath of the Lamb,* ¹⁷ for the great day of their *wrath* has come, and who can stand?" (Rev 6:15–17)

Also see:

> The nations raged, but *your wrath came,* and the time for the dead to be judged, and for rewarding your servants, the prophets and saints, and those who fear your name, both small and great, *and for destroying the destroyers of the earth.* (Rev 11:18)

Furthermore, when the third angel pours out his bowl of the wrath of God on fresh waters, the angel in charge declares that the punishments are just, because the world shed the blood of saints and prophets:

> The third angel poured out his bowl into the rivers and the springs of water, and they became blood. ⁵ And I heard the angel in charge of the waters say,
> "Just are you, O Holy One, who is and who was,
>   for you brought these judgments.
> ⁶ For they have shed the blood of saints and prophets,
>   and you have given them blood to drink.
> It is what they deserve!" (Rev 16:4–6)

The many theories of rapture usually emanate from readers not understanding this difference between tribulation and wrath. By lumping the two separate events, many have used the following verse to justify their position that Christians will not experience the great tribulation:

> For God has not destined us for wrath, but to obtain salvation through our Lord Jesus Christ, ¹⁰ who died for us so that whether we are awake or asleep we might live with him. (1 Thess 5:9–10)

However, as can be seen from relevant biblical texts, the great tribulation is not the wrath of God. The wrath of God will mainly target those who persecuted Christians. By the time the wrath of God is unleashed, many Christians will have been martyred, in hiding, or in prison and hence will not experience the wrath.

Jesus Christ clearly stated that Christians will be delivered unto tribulation:

> *"Then they will deliver you up to tribulation and put you to death,*
> and you will be hated by all nations for my name's sake. (Matt 24:9)

Many Christians will face the antichrist, because they will be on earth when the identity of the antichrist will be revealed, and the abomination of desolation happens:

> "So when you see the abomination of desolation spoken of by the prophet Daniel, standing in the holy place (let the reader understand), [16] then let those who are in Judea flee to the mountains. [17] Let the one who is on the housetop not go down to take what is in his house, [18] and let the one who is in the field not turn back to take his cloak. [19] And alas for women who are pregnant and for those who are nursing infants in those days! [20] Pray that your flight may not be in winter or on a Sabbath. [21] *For then there will be great tribulation*, such as has not been from the beginning of the world until now, no, and never will be. [22] And if those days had not been cut short, no human being would be saved. *But for the sake of the elect those days will be cut short.* [23] Then if anyone says to you, 'Look, here is the Christ!' or 'There he is!' do not believe it. [24] For false christs and false prophets will arise and perform great signs and wonders, so as to lead astray, if possible, even the elect. [25] See, I have told you beforehand. [26] So, if they say to you, 'Look, he is in the wilderness,' do not go out. If they say, 'Look, he is in the inner rooms,' do not believe it. [27] For as the lightning comes from the east and shines as far as the west, so will be the coming of the Son of Man. [28] Wherever the corpse is, there the vultures will gather. (Matt 24:15–28)

He reiterated this by pointing out that his coming will be after the tribulation. Hence, some Christians (those not martyred) will be on earth when he comes—"See, I have told you beforehand" (Matt 24:25).

This was also captured by St. Paul in his Second Letter to Thessalonians:

> Now concerning the coming of our Lord Jesus Christ and our being gathered together to him, we ask you, brothers, [2] not to be quickly shaken in mind or alarmed, either by a spirit or a spoken word, or a letter seeming to be from us, to the effect that the day of the Lord has come. [3] Let no one deceive you in any way. For that day will not come, unless the rebellion comes first, and the man of lawlessness is revealed, the son of destruction, [4] who opposes and exalts himself against every so-called god or object of worship, so that he takes his seat in the temple of God, proclaiming himself to be God. (2 Thess 2:1–4)

The rebellion that St. Paul is referring to here is the falling away of many Christians from the faith that Jesus Christ mentioned. The man of lawlessness is the antichrist. His taking up "his seat in the temple of God, proclaiming himself to be God" points to the abomination of desolation that Christ pointed out for us to watch out for.

This *coming of Christ* that Paul is referring to is the second coming of Christ, when Jesus will come to fight and defeat the antichrist at the battle of Armageddon (see §6.6.2), which happens after the tribulation:

> And then the lawless one will be revealed, whom the Lord Jesus will kill with the breath of his mouth and bring to nothing by the appearance of *his coming*. (2 Thess 2:8)

Therefore, St. Paul is not referring to a hidden event (rapture) when Jesus Christ will first come to extract Christians, as is purported by some Bible scholars, and then come back again to fight antichrist and establish his millennial kingdom.

Thus, according to St. Paul, Jesus Christ will not come until the antichrist is revealed and the abomination of desolation happens. However, note that Jesus Christ admonished his followers to flee to the mountains when the abomination of desolation happens and not to wait to be raptured:

> "So when you see the abomination of desolation spoken of by the prophet Daniel, standing in the holy place (let the reader understand), [16] then let those who are in Judea flee to the mountains. (Matt 24:15–16)

Furthermore, the great multitude who are seen at the opening of the sixth seal were martyred (see §4.11). Although many Bible translations describe them as "those coming out of the great tribulation" (Rev 7:14), the New Living Translation translates "coming out" as "died":

> Then he said to me, "These are the ones who died in the great tribulation. They have washed their robes in the blood of the Lamb and made them white. (Rev 7:14 NLT)

Had they not undergone tribulation, they wouldn't have been killed by the enemy of God. In conclusion, Christians will go through the great tribulation. There are various pointers in the Bible (including direct quotes of Jesus Christ) that lead one to this conclusion.

2

Letters to the Seven Churches

2.1. FINAL CALL BEFORE THE TROUBLES—ANALYZING THE LETTERS TO THE SEVEN CHURCHES

> John to the seven churches that are in Asia: Grace to you and peace from him who is and who was and who is to come, and from the seven spirits who are before his throne, [5] and from Jesus Christ the faithful witness, the firstborn of the dead, and the ruler of kings on earth. To him who loves us and has freed us from our sins by his blood [6] and made us a kingdom, priests to his God and Father, to him be glory and dominion forever and ever. Amen. [7] Behold, he is coming with the clouds, and every eye will see him, even those who pierced him, and all tribes of the earth will wail on account of him. Even so. Amen. [8] "I am the Alpha and the Omega," says the Lord God, "who is and who was and who is to come, the Almighty." (Rev 1:4–8)

At the beginning of the revelation of the events of the end-time, Christ sends letters to seven churches scattered across the Asia Minor (modern-day Turkey[1]). In these letters, he provides what could be viewed as feedback or a scorecard on the spiritual status of the churches.

---

1. Rivera, "7 Churches of Revelation."

The letters have been a subject of discussion by many Bible scholars, with each school of thought proffering different interpretations.[2] Summarized are the attributes/hidden meaning of the churches:

- Ephesus: The church that had abandoned its first love for Christ (Rev 2:4)
- Smyrna: The church that would face severe persecution (Rev 2:10)
- Pergamum: The church that needed to repent of sin (Rev 2:16)
- Thyatira: The church whose false prophetess was leading people astray (Rev 2:20)
- Sardis: The sleeping church that needed to wake up (Rev 3:2)
- Philadelphia: The church that had patiently persevered (Rev 3:10)
- Laodicea: The church with lukewarm faith (Rev 3:16)

Other authors have also interpreted the seven churches to symbolize the chronological history of the Christian church, with each church representing a period in church history[3]:

1. The Apostolic Church ≈ AD 30–300
2. The Martyr Church ≈ AD 100–313
3. The Compromising Church ≈ AD 314–590
4. The Roman Catholic Church ≈ AD 590–1517
5. The Reformation Church ≈ AD 1517–1700
6. The Revival Church ≈ AD 1700–1900
7. The Worldly Church ≈ AD 1900–rapture

The letters have also been viewed by many as letters sent to the churches during the time of John and having no relationship to the other events in the book of Revelation. This is due to the fact that the seven churches were actually existing with physical congregations at the time John wrote the book of Revelation (around AD 95).

Despite various interpretations and opinions about this, the only interpretation that seems to be valid in the current dispensation is the perspective that the seven churches represent the state of affairs among a generation of Christians that would be on earth close to the time of the great tribulation. There are various contents of the letters that clearly point

---

2. Fairchild, "Meaning of the 7 Churches."
3. Verrett, "What Is the Significance."

towards the end-time. Many scholars believe that apart from being directed at the seven churches in existence then, the letters have a second, hidden meaning directed at the Christian church that will be in existence just before the events of the end-time commences. This sort of hidden meaning is replicated in many prophecies and verses across the Bible—the dualism of prophecy. It is obvious that the letters were also addressed to a generation of Christians that will be in the world close to the end-time (the generation that will witness the great tribulation), and not only for a generation of Christians at the time of John. Otherwise, there was no need for the letters to contain pointers to the end-time (the persecutions and tribulation), when all the contemporary recipients would all be dead without witnessing the end-time.

The letters are akin to Christ sending a final assessment of the state of the churches before the events of the end-time unfold. In the letter he x-rays the activities of the churches—where each church is getting it right and where it is not. The letters also serve as a final warning to the churches to sit up and put their houses in order before the storm arrives.

In this light, the seven churches do not represent only the specific seven churches in Asia Minor at the time John got the vision but also represent seven classes/sets of Christians that will be in the world just before the end-time events unfold. Churches were specifically used to reiterate that the letters are for Christians and not for other religions that will be present in the world at this time. It is also important to note that despite several churches that were in existence at the time John received the revelation, including the big churches in Corinth and Antioch, the letters were addressed only to seven minor churches situated closest to Patmos, where John was exiled.[4]

It should be assumed that the characteristics of the churches portrayed in the letters were present in the selected churches at that time, thus relevant to their time. However, in the wider context, each of those churches was representative of the nature of the Christian church towards the end-time. Even though there are more than seven churches at the time Christ sent the letters, it was addressed to only seven, as if Jesus were oblivious of other churches. This may indicate that despite multifarious Christian church denominations that will be existing towards the end-time, Christ will recognize only seven types of Christians across the various denominations, with each group having a characteristic represented by one of the churches. The use of seven churches also follows the rule of sevens used across the various phases of the revelation (see §1.4).

---

4. Jeremiah, "Seven Churches of Revelation"; Rivera, "7 Churches of Revelation."

As a final call for repentance, it seems that this will be most relevant during the precursor periods when the white horse rider appears on the scene and persecution of Christians is commencing.

There is no doubt that many Christians today have wandered from biblical truths and sound doctrines, some have become lukewarm, others have become lovers of pleasure, a large proportion have been drawn to prosperity gospels, while others are abandoning core tenets of Christianity to accommodate cultures and practices of the modern society, in order to blend with the politically correct bandwagon. And if the church goes into the great tribulation in this spiritual state, many souls will be lost.

The following sections will attempt to analyze the contents of each letter, to decipher the key message in them and how they apply to the present generation.

2.2. LETTER TO THE CHURCH IN EPHESUS

To the angel of the church in Ephesus write: "The words of him who holds the seven stars in his right hand, who walks among the seven golden lampstands.² ¹I know your works, your toil and your patient endurance, and how you cannot bear with those who are evil, but have tested those who call themselves apostles and are not, and found them to be false. ³I know you are enduring patiently and bearing up for my name's sake, and you have not grown weary. ⁴But I have this against you, that you have abandoned the love you had at first. ⁵Remember therefore from where you have fallen; repent, and do the works you did at first. If not, I will come to you and remove your lampstand from its place, unless you repent. ⁶Yet this you have: you hate the works of the Nicolaitans, which I also hate. ⁷He who has an ear, let him hear what the Spirit says to the churches. To the one who conquers I will grant to eat of the tree of life, which is in the paradise of God.'" (Rev 2:1–8).

The attributes of the church in Ephesus tend to describe the set of Christians who could generally be referred to as good Christians with right doctrine ("cannot bear with those who are evil" and "hate the works of the Nicolaitans"), discerning (ability to detect false prophets), zealously toiling and working for God's kingdom ("your works, your toil and your patient endurance" and "enduring patiently and bearing up for my name's sake"). However, it appears the intolerance of this set of Christians may have hardened their hearts against others not zealously pursuing the work of God. This may have made them judgmental and less charitable. It appears that the agape love found among early adherents of Christianity may have waned from this set of Christians ("you have abandoned the love you had at first"). Hence, the warning from Christ to them to repent and retrace their steps.

The reward for this set of Christians who conquers the trials of the period (possibly the persecution of Christians during the end-time—the great tribulation) will be the privilege to eat from the tree of life. This tree of life that is in the paradise of God is possibly the same tree of life found in the new Jerusalem:

> Then the angel showed me the river of the water of life, bright as crystal, flowing from the throne of God and of the Lamb ² through the middle of the street of the city; also, on either side of the river, the tree of life with its twelve kinds of fruit, yielding its fruit each month. (Rev 22:1–2)

This suggests that those Christians who conquer will be assured a seat in the new Jerusalem that will be set up after Satan and his followers have been sent to the lake of fire. It is instructive to note that those who will be found in the new Jerusalem are those who made it through the first resurrection (§6.7).

2.2.1. Who are the Nicolaitans?

The Nicolaitans were followers of Nicholas of Antioch, who was among the seven deacons chosen alongside Stephen to ease the burden of serving the congregation of the early Christians:

> And what they said pleased the whole gathering, and they chose Stephen, a man full of faith and of the Holy Spirit, and Philip, and Prochorus, and Nicanor, and Timon, and Parmenas, and Nicolaus, a proselyte of Antioch. ⁶ These they set before the apostles, and they prayed and laid their hands on them. (Acts 6:5–7)

Nicolaitans were among the many heretical Christian sects with roots in Gnosticism, whose doctrines infiltrated the early Christian churches such as those at Ephesus and at Pergamum. Irenaeus[5] identified them as men

---

5. "Irenaeus (ca. 125–202) was bishop of Lugdunum in Gaul, which is now Lyons, France. Irenaeus was born in Smyrna in Asia Minor, where he studied under bishop Polycarp, who in turn had been a disciple of the Apostle John. Leaving Asia Minor for Rome he joined the school of Justin Martyr before being made bishop of Lyons in Southern Gaul in about 178 AD. Irenaeus is primarily noted for his refutation of early Gnosticism. To this end he wrote his major work *Against Heresies*, in which [he] also

who "lead lives of unrestrained indulgence."[6] The Nicolaitans teach that it is a matter of indifference to practise adultery, and to eat things sacrificed to idols. "Nicolaitans of the 2nd century seem to have continued and extended the views of the 1st century adherents, holding to the freedom of the flesh and sin, and teaching that the deeds of the flesh had no effect upon the health of the soul and consequently no relation to salvation."[7] This doctrine is like the doctrine that Balaam used to lure Israelites to sin against God (see §2.4.1).

2.3. LETTER TO THE CHURCH IN SMYRNA

> And to the angel of the church in Smyrna write: "The words of the first and the last, who died and came to life. [9] 'I know your tribulation and your poverty (but you are rich) and the slander of those who say that they are Jews and are not, but are a synagogue of Satan. [10] Do not fear what you are about to suffer. Behold, the devil is about to throw some of you into prison, that you may be tested, and for ten days you will have tribulation. Be faithful unto death, and I will give you the crown of life. [11] He who has an ear, let him hear what the Spirit says to the churches. The one who conquers will not be hurt by the second death." (Rev 2:8–11)

The church in Smyrna seems to portray the attributes of Christians during the end-time who will be fearless and outspoken like Stephen (Acts 7) in preaching the gospel of our Lord Jesus Christ. This group of Christians will undergo hardship, slander, persecution, and tribulation: "I know your tribulation and your poverty."

It seems this group of Christians will be spearheading the bearing of witness for Christ at the beginning of persecution of Christians. Some will be killed; some will be punished severely and imprisoned:

> But before all these things, they will lay their hands on you and persecute you, delivering you up to the synagogues and prisons. You will be brought before kings and rulers for My name's sake. [13] But it will turn out for you as an occasion for testimony. [14] Therefore settle it in your hearts not to meditate beforehand on what you will answer; [15] for I will give you a

---

sought to expound and defend the orthodox Christian faith" (Theopedia, "Irenaeus").

6. Iranaeus, *Against Heresies*, bk. 1, ch. 26, as quoted in Theopedia, "Nicolaitans."
7. Theopedia, "Nicolaitans."

mouth and wisdom which all your adversaries will not be able to contradict or resist. ¹⁶ You will be betrayed even by parents and brothers, relatives and friends; and they will put some of you to death. ¹⁷ And you will be hated by all for My name's sake. ¹⁸ But not a hair of your head shall be lost. ¹⁹ By your patience possess your souls. (Luke 21:12–19–NKJV)

Just like Stephen, these may make up the bulk of Christians that will be martyred at the beginning of the persecutions of the end-time (during the precursor periods—second seal to fifth seal). They are most likely among the martyrs seen at the opening of the fifth seal:

> When he opened the fifth seal, I saw under the altar the souls of those who had been slain for the word of God and for the witness they had borne. (Rev 6:9)

These Christians will be among those to rise at the first resurrection after the battle of Armageddon, when Christ is establishing his millennial reign on earth, because they will not undergo the second death ("the one who conquers will not be hurt by the second death"):

> Then I saw thrones, and seated on them were those to whom the authority to judge was committed. Also I saw the souls of those who had been beheaded for the testimony of Jesus and for the word of God, and those who had not worshiped the beast or its image and had not received its mark on their foreheads or their hands. They came to life and reigned with Christ for a thousand years. ⁵ The rest of the dead did not come to life until the thousand years were ended. This is the first resurrection. ⁶ *Blessed and holy is the one who shares in the first resurrection! Over such the second death has no power,* but they will be priests of God and of Christ, and they will reign with him for a thousand years. (Rev 20:4–7)

To buttress this point, the letter was introduced with Jesus Christ describing himself as "the first and the last, who died and came to life." This tends to serve as a reminder that those who died in Christ will eventually come to life. Hence, it is a way to reassure this set of Christians that even if they die during the tribulation, they will be resurrected at the end.

2.3.1. Who Are the Modern-Day Synagogue of Satan?

Many Jews were very hostile to the early Christians. There were also conflicts simmering underneath between Jewish Christians and the gentile converts to Christianity whom St. Paul assured that they became Jews in spirit. Furthermore, there were other Jewish sects such as the Hypsistarians[8] who did not agree with certain Christian doctrines, even though they accepted and practiced a few others in common with Christians. These may have formed the group that Christ was referring to as the synagogue of Satan at the time the letter was delivered.

However, in contemporary times and towards the beginning of tribulations of the end-time, it seems there will be a set of religious people (perhaps with Judeo-Christian background) who will claim to be Jews, when in actual sense they are not. These individuals will adopt a high moral ground in the claim of being the chosen children of God and ferociously slander/attack Christians, especially those from gentile nations, whom they will perceive as being inferior to them, in terms of the things of God. Currently, there are various Christian religious groups, especially popular among African Americans, who tend to claim they are the original Jews scattered across the world that will be restored to their original land of Israel shortly before Christ returns. These may form what Christ is referring to as the synagogue of Satan, relevant to the end-time.

In addition, there are also various Jewish sects in Israel who are tirelessly working to restore the temple at Jerusalem and commence daily sacrifice in the temple. Daniel hinted that such a ceremony will initially be allowed by the antichrist in the beginning, but this will be stopped midway, and the abomination of desolation will be set up:

> He shall turn back and pay attention to those who forsake the holy covenant. [31] Forces from him shall appear and profane the temple and fortress, and shall take away the regular burnt offering. And they shall set up the abomination that makes desolate. (Dan 11:30–31)

This group of Jews, who are obviously not Christians, will believe they have restored the worship of God, not understanding that the death of Christ on the cross has superseded the usual sacrifice prescribed in the Old Testament. This will result in conflict between such sects and Christians, and they could be the group being referred to as the synagogue of Satan. No doubt that the true identities of this group of people will become clearer closer to the time.

---

8. Arendzen, "Hypsistarians."

2.4. LETTER TO THE CHURCH IN PERGAMUM

> And to the angel of the church in Pergamum write: "The words of him who has the sharp two-edged sword. [13] 'I know where you dwell, where Satan's throne is. Yet you hold fast my name, and you did not deny my faith even in the days of Antipas my faithful witness, who was killed among you, where Satan dwells. [14] But I have a few things against you: you have some there who hold the teaching of Balaam, who taught Balak to put a stumbling block before the sons of Israel, so that they might eat food sacrificed to idols and practice sexual immorality. [15] So also you have some who hold the teaching of the Nicolaitans. [16] Therefore repent. If not, I will come to you soon and war against them with the sword of my mouth. [17] He who has an ear, let him hear what the Spirit says to the churches. To the one who conquers I will give some of the hidden manna, and I will give him a white stone, with a new name written on the stone that no one knows except the one who receives it." (Rev 2:12–18)

The church in Pergamum might be describing the attributes of a group of Christians towards the end-time who will strongly believe in God and Jesus Christ. They will demonstrate strength in the faith during initial persecutions of Christians. However, despite their strength, they accommodate two dangerous and bad doctrines: the teachings of Balaam and the Nicolaitans. These doctrines that are concerned with idolatry (food sacrificed to idols) and sexual immorality are abhorred by Jesus.

These doctrines might affect contemporary Christians who believe they are immune to sin by God's grace. Especially susceptible are adherents of the doctrine of "once saved, always saved" who misapply this to mean that they can indulge in any form of sexual immorality and some forms of idolatry without repercussions, because they have been saved and covered by grace. Such Christians could easily be led astray by false doctrines that cause them to stumble in faith, just as Balaam showed Balak how to make Israelites to defile themselves so that God can punish them.

The apostle Jude warned against these:

> For certain people have crept in unnoticed who long ago were designated for this condemnation, ungodly people, who pervert the grace of our God into sensuality and deny our only Master and Lord, Jesus Christ. [5] Now I want to remind you, although you once fully knew it, that Jesus, who saved a people out of the land of Egypt, afterward destroyed those who did not believe. [6] And the angels who did not stay within their own

> position of authority, but left their proper dwelling, he has kept in eternal chains under gloomy darkness until the judgment of the great day— ⁷ just as Sodom and Gomorrah and the surrounding cities, which likewise indulged in sexual immorality and pursued unnatural desire, serve as an example by undergoing a punishment of eternal fire. (Jude 1:4–7)

The teachings of Balaam led to Israelites committing sexual immorality with Moabite women, which made them commit idolatry (see §2.4.1). The Nicolaitans believed that the acts of the flesh did not impact one's salvation, hence, they encouraged indulgence in all sorts of sexual immorality.

Hence, the church in Pergamum is representative of Christians whose relationship with God will be eroded as they are tempted by many false doctrines that will be in place during the end-time. These Christians can withstand persecutions ("did not deny my faith even in the days of Antipas my faithful witness, who was killed among you"), but some of them will fall prey to subtle, deceptive, and seductive doctrines that will creep into the churches and could lead such Christians astray.

Christ is warning against these, as he will treat those who do not repent of this, the same way he will treat the antichrist and followers:

> If not, I will come to you soon and war against them with the sword of my mouth. (Rev 2:16).

Recall that Christ introduces himself in this letter as "him who has the sharp two-edged sword." This matches the description of the rider of the white horse who comes to make war against the antichrist and his army at the battle of Armageddon:

> Then I saw heaven opened, and behold, a white horse! The one sitting on it is called Faithful and True, and in righteousness he judges and makes war. ¹² His eyes are like a flame of fire, and on his head are many diadems, and he has a name written that no one knows but himself. ¹³ He is clothed in a robe dipped in blood, and the name by which he is called is The Word of God. ¹⁴ And the armies of heaven, arrayed in fine linen, white and pure, were following him on white horses. ¹⁵ From his mouth comes a sharp sword with which to strike down the nations, and he will rule them with a rod of iron. He will tread the winepress of the fury of the wrath of God the Almighty. (Rev 19:11–15)

The Christians who will conquer the temptation of the false doctrines will be cared for by Christ during the hard times. They might be provided with food and new identities during the great tribulation:

> To the one who conquers I will give some of the hidden manna, and I will give him a white stone, with a new name written on the stone that no one knows except the one who receives it. (Rev 2:17)

2.4.1. What Is the Teaching of Balaam?

To understand this passage on the teaching of Balaam, one needs to go back to the book of Numbers (chs 22–25), where the story of the encounter between the Israelites and Midianites at the plains of Moab is relayed.

The story could be summarized thus: while the Israelites were sojourning in the wilderness, after leaving Egypt, they were conquering nations on their path to the promise land. On getting close to the land of the Midianites, the kings of the lands under Balak (king of Moab), having realized they cannot face the Israelites in battle, decided to use spiritual means to combat them. They decided to hire Balaam, a prophet ("he hears from God"), whose "way was perverse" (Num 22:32) to curse the Israelites. However, every effort Balaam made to curse them backfired, and instead of cursing them, he blessed them. This infuriated the Midianite kings, who had paid him heavily for this failed task. Thus, Balaam, recognizing that no one could curse the Israelites, devised a wicked strategy that would make the Israelites bring a curse upon themselves. His idea was simple: get the Israelites to disobey God through sin that will anger him to punish them. The Midianites were advised to use their women to lure Israel to sin. The Israelites fell for this honeytrap and indulged in sexual immorality with Midianite women (committing fornication with Midianite women), which ultimately led them into idolatry with Midianite gods (worshiping Baal of Peor), thus causing the anger of God to rage against them:

> While Israel lived in Shittim, the people began to whore with the daughters of Moab. ² These invited the people to the sacrifices of their gods, and the people ate and bowed down to their gods. ³ So Israel yoked himself to Baal of Peor. And the anger of the Lord was kindled against Israel. (Num 25:1–3)

This caused a plague that resulted in the death of twenty-four thousand people:

> And the Lord said to Moses, "Take all the chiefs of the people and hang them in the sun before the Lord, that the fierce anger of the Lord may turn away from Israel." ⁵ And Moses said to the judges of Israel, "Each of you kill those of his men who have

yoked themselves to Baal of Peor." ⁶ And behold, one of the people of Israel came and brought a Midianite woman to his family, in the sight of Moses and in the sight of the whole congregation of the people of Israel, while they were weeping in the entrance of the tent of meeting. ⁷ When Phinehas the son of Eleazar, son of Aaron the priest, saw it, he rose and left the congregation and took a spear in his hand ⁸ and went after the man of Israel into the chamber and pierced both of them, the man of Israel and the woman through her belly. Thus, the plague on the people of Israel was stopped. ⁹ Nevertheless, those who died by the plague were twenty-four thousand. (Num 25:1–12)

Although it was not explicitly stated in Numbers when Balaam taught the Midianites this devious trick, Moses hinted at this teaching of Balaam when he expressed his shock and ire that Israelite soldiers who went to revenge the Midianites for bringing the curse of God upon them spared the women. Even though they killed all Midianite kings, their males and Balaam, they spared the women, and Moses did not like the idea. Moses was outraged because it was through the women that sexual immorality had crept into the camp of Israelites and yoked them with Baal-Peor:

> Moses said to them, "Have you let all the women live? ¹⁶ Behold, these, on Balaam's advice, caused the people of Israel to act treacherously against the LORD in the incident of Peor, and so the plague came among the congregation of the LORD. ¹⁷ Now therefore, kill every male among the little ones, and kill every woman who has known man by lying with him. ¹⁸ But all the young girls who have not known man by lying with him keep alive for yourselves. (Num 31:15–18)

2.5. LETTER TO THE CHURCH IN THYATIRA

And to the angel of the church in Thyatira write: "The words of the Son of God, who has eyes like a flame of fire, and whose feet are like burnished bronze. ¹⁹ 'I know your works, your love and faith and service and patient endurance, and that your latter works exceed the first. ²⁰ But I have this against you, that you tolerate that woman Jezebel, who calls herself a prophetess and is teaching and seducing my servants to practice sexual immorality and to eat food sacrificed to idols. ²¹ I gave her time to repent, but she refuses to repent of her sexual immorality. ²² Behold, I will throw her onto a sickbed, and those who commit adultery with her I will throw into great tribulation, unless they repent of her works, ²³ and I will strike her children dead. And all the churches will know that I am he who searches mind and heart, and I will give to each of you according to your works. ²⁴ But to the rest of you in Thyatira, who do not hold this teaching, who have not learned what some call the deep things of Satan, to you I say, I do not lay on you any other burden. ²⁵ Only hold fast what you have until I come. ²⁶ The one who conquers and who keeps my works until the end, to him I will give authority over the nations, ²⁷ and he will rule them with a rod of iron, as when earthen pots are broken in pieces, even as I myself have received authority from my Father. ²⁸ And I will give him the morning star. ²⁹ He who has an ear, let him hear what the Spirit says to the churches.'" (Rev 2:18–29)

Jezebel was a foreign (Phoenician) princess who married Ahab, one of Israel's notorious kings. She was a high priestess of Baal and an ardent worshipper of Ashtaroth (Baal's female counterpart). Hence, she had a goal of replacing the worship of God in Israel with the worship of Baal and Ashtaroth. This resulted in her having constant confrontation with the true prophets of God, including Elijah. She ended up slaughtering many prophets in Israel, whom she replaced with prophets of Baal, and forcing others, including Elijah, into hiding. Hence, Jezebel represents a purveyor/facilitator of false religion or idolatry. In the letter to Thyatira, Jesus Christ mentions a woman who claims to be a prophetess but whom Christ sees as Jezebel:

> But I have this against you, that you tolerate that woman Jezebel, who calls herself a prophetess and is teaching and seducing my servants to practice sexual immorality and to eat food sacrificed to idols. ²¹ I gave her time to repent, but she refuses to repent of her sexual immorality. (Rev 2:20–21)

This could be an individual among the followers of Christ. As at the time the letter was delivered, such a woman teaching the congregation might have existed. However, this may also symbolize something else, especially for the church during the end-time. Thus, the woman could represent a false religion that will rear its head towards the end-time to stifle the true worship of God. It is important to note that this letter points towards the end-time, as Christ warns that he will throw those who tolerate this woman into the great tribulation.

> Behold, I will throw her onto a sickbed, and those who commit adultery with her I will throw into great tribulation, unless they repent of her works, ²³ and I will strike her children dead. And

> all the churches will know that I am he who searches mind and heart, and I will give to each of you according to your works. (Rev 2:22–23)

The Jezebel referred to in this letter could be the New Age movement[9] or more outrageous pseudo-Christian religious movements that will be in the world just before the great tribulation. The New Age movement is a counterfeit of Christianity that worships the devil, in the same manner Jezebel counterfeited the true worship of God by substituting God with Baal.

Hence, the church in Thyatira may represent Christians that will be misled by wrong doctrines of false prophets/prophetesses of the end-time, who will entice them with "deep revelations" that will actually lead them to the doctrines of Satan. Already, such prophetic ministries are becoming rampant across Christian communities globally. Such Christians who do not repent from such doctrines will be among the Christians that will be consumed during the great tribulation and possibly may not resurrect during the first resurrection:

It also seems that the rest of the Christians in this subgroup referred to as the church in Thyatira will still be on earth when Christ comes and will be given authority to rule over nations:

> But to the rest of you in Thyatira, who do not hold this teaching, who have not learned what some call the deep things of Satan, to you I say, I do not lay on you any other burden. ^{25} Only hold fast what you have until I come. ^{26} The one who conquers and who keeps my works until the end, to him I will give authority over the nations, ^{27} and he will rule them with a rod of iron, as when earthen pots are broken in pieces, even as I myself have received authority from my Father. (Rev 2:24–27)

However, since Christ makes a distinction between the members of this church that will go into the great tribulation and those that should endure to the end, it seems they will be kept somewhere on earth where they won't directly be touched by the troubles of the great tribulation.

This set of Christians, having endured the hardship of the world and antichrist during the great tribulation and having survived all the troubles of the time, will have demonstrated resilience and justly earned the authority with which they will be bestowed. A reference to this authority to those Christians who survive the times is made while describing the first resurrection:

---

9. Melton, "New Age Movement."

> Then I saw thrones, and seated on them were those to whom the authority to judge was committed. Also I saw the souls of those who had been beheaded for the testimony of Jesus and for the word of God, and those who had not worshiped the beast or its image and had not received its mark on their foreheads or their hands. They came to life and reigned with Christ for a thousand years. (Rev 20:4)

Perhaps this set of Christians on earth will be different from those who went into the "wilderness," because those in the wilderness will be nourished, whereas those in the secular world with others will endure the hardship. The sickbed referred to in this passage might be the pestilence of the end-time—fourth seal.

2.6. LETTER TO THE CHURCH IN SARDIS

> And to the angel of the church in Sardis write: "The words of him who has the seven spirits of God and the seven stars. 'I know your works. You have the reputation of being alive, but you are dead. ² Wake up, and strengthen what remains and is about to die, for I have not found your works complete in the sight of my God. ³ Remember, then, what you received and heard. Keep it, and repent. If you will not wake up, I will come like a thief, and you will not know at what hour I will come against you. ⁴ Yet you have still a few names in Sardis, people who have not soiled their garments, and they will walk with me in white, for they are worthy. ⁵ The one who conquers will be clothed thus in white garments, and I will never blot his name out of the book of life. I will confess his name before my Father and before his angels. ⁶ He who has an ear, let him hear what the Spirit says to the churches.'"(Rev 3:1–6)

The church in Sardis represents drowsy Christians, who think they are in the right with God ("being alive") but will be taken by surprise by the events of the end-time. Many in this subgroup will not see it coming if they don't wake up:

> If you will not wake up, I will come like a thief, and you will not know at what hour I will come against you. (Rev 3:3)

The admonishment of Jesus Christ in the Gospels for Christians to always stay awake and pray so that they can escape the trials of the great tribulation, is apt for this group of Christians::

> But watch yourselves lest your hearts be weighed down with dissipation and drunkenness and cares of this life, and that day come upon you suddenly like a trap. ³⁵ For it will come upon all who dwell on the face of the whole earth. ³⁶ But stay awake at all times, praying that you may have strength to escape all these things that are going to take place, and to stand before the Son of Man. (Luke 21:34–36)

From the passage, it seems that this set of Christians will experience the persecutions of the great tribulation. And many of them will be martyred during the great tribulation for the testimony of Christ and hence will be given white garments:

> Yet you have still a few names in Sardis, people who have not soiled their garments, and they will walk with me in white, for they are worthy. ⁵ The one who conquers will be clothed thus in white garments, and I will never blot his name out of the book of life. (Rev 3:4–5)

These might be among the martyrs found at the opening of the fifth seal and among the great multitude found after the opening of the sixth seal, who came out from the great tribulation.

2.7. LETTER TO THE CHURCH IN PHILADELPHIA

> And to the angel of the church in Philadelphia write: "The words of the holy one, the true one, who has the key of David, who opens and no one will shut, who shuts and no one opens.⁸ 'I know your works. Behold, I have set before you an open door, which no one is able to shut. I know that you have but little power, and yet you have kept my word and have not denied my name. ⁹ Behold, I will make those of the synagogue of Satan who say that they are Jews and are not, but lie—behold, I will make them come and bow down before your feet, and they will learn that I have loved you. ¹⁰ Because you have kept my word about patient endurance, I will keep you from the hour of trial that is coming on the whole world, to try those who dwell on the earth. ¹¹ I am coming soon. Hold fast what you have, so that no one may seize your crown. ¹² The one who conquers, I will make him a pillar in the temple of my God. Never shall he go out of it, and I will write on him the name of my God, and the name of the city of my God, the new Jerusalem, which comes down from my God out of heaven, and my own new name. ¹³ He who

has an ear, let him hear what the Spirit says to the churches.'"
(Rev 3:7–13)

Key attributes of the church in Philadelphia include the following: not being powerful, keeping Christ's words, not denying Christ's name when it mattered most:

> I know that you have but little power, and yet you have kept my word and have not denied my name. (Rev 3:8)

Jesus Christ specifically notes their patient endurance:

> Because you have kept my word about patient endurance (Rev 3:10)

This church in Philadelphia may represent the most faithful Christians during the birth pains period. They will understand the time because they are very awake and have been watching for the signs, hence they will know that the events of the end-time have commenced. It seems these Christians who will survive the initial persecution of Satan, which will intensify during the fifth seal period, will be protected from the great tribulation:

> Behold, I have set before you an open door, which no one is able to shut. (Rev 3:8)

> Because you have kept my word about patient endurance, I will keep you from the hour of trial that is coming on the whole world, to try those who dwell on the earth. (Rev 3:10).

Perhaps they will be taken to the wilderness (see §4.5), to preserve them from the coming great tribulation.

2.8. TO THE CHURCH IN LAODICEA

> And to the angel of the church in Laodicea write: "The words of the Amen, the faithful and true witness, the beginning of God's creation. [15] 'I know your works: you are neither cold nor hot. Would that you were either cold or hot! [16] So, because you are lukewarm, and neither hot nor cold, I will spit you out of my mouth. [17] For you say, I am rich, I have prospered, and I need nothing, not realizing that you are wretched, pitiable, poor, blind, and naked. [18] I counsel you to buy from me gold refined by fire, so that you may be rich, and white garments so that you may clothe yourself and the shame of your nakedness may not be seen, and salve to anoint your eyes, so that you may

see. ¹⁹ Those whom I love, I reprove and discipline, so be zealous and repent. ²⁰ Behold, I stand at the door and knock. If anyone hears my voice and opens the door, I will come in to him and eat with him, and he with me. ²¹ The one who conquers, I will grant him to sit with me on my throne, as I also conquered and sat down with my Father on his throne. ²² He who has an ear, let him hear what the Spirit says to the churches.'" (Rev 3:14–22)

The church in Laodicea represents the group of Christians, who will initially seek to preserve their lives from the end-time persecutions, either by staying neutral/politically correct or shying away from openly bearing witness for Christ. They may also be those Christians who were not watching and praying and failed to recognize the time. The Laodicean church will also encompass prosperous and wealthy Christians who may have been imbued with the prosperity gospel and hence not motivated to bear witness for Christ at the time of persecution:

> For you say, I am rich, I have prospered, and I need nothing, not realizing that you are wretched, pitiable, poor, blind, and naked. (Rev 3:17)

This set of Christians can redeem themselves only by embracing the great tribulation and paying the necessary price. By the time the antichrist rolls out its actions, such as the mark of the beast (666), these Christians who are familiar with end-time theology will realize that it has eventually started.

Christ is actually admonishing them to accept the great tribulation as a means to cleanse and save themselves from damnation:

> I counsel you to buy from me gold refined by fire, so that you may be rich, and white garments so that you may clothe yourself and the shame of your nakedness may not be seen, and salve to anoint your eyes, so that you may see. ¹⁹ Those whom I love, I reprove and discipline, so be zealous and repent. (Rev 3:18–19)

They will realize that they may have missed the mark, and many of them will work to make heaven. The only ones who will make heaven will be those who refuse to worship the beast, hence will be imprisoned and/or beheaded or killed in another form. This is the only way they will wash their clothes clean. These will probably be among the multitudes from every nation and tribe found at the throne of God:

> These are the ones coming out of the great tribulation. They have washed their robes and made them white in the blood of the Lamb." (Rev 7:14)

Hence, Christ is not precluding this set of Christians from salvation:

> ²⁰Behold, I stand at the door and knock. If anyone hears my voice and opens the door, I will come into him and eat with him, and he with me. ²¹ The one who conquers, I will grant him to sit with me on my throne, as I also conquered and sat down with my Father on his throne. (Rev 3:20-21)

Jesus Christ will allow this set of Christians to go through the great tribulation so as to refine them and clothe them in white garments. Due to his love for them, he will not permit them to perish but give them a second chance to sit up and repent.

Take note from the foregoing that this set of Christians is called to repent. They are expected to be refined by fire and conquer, just as Christ conquered—through his death on the cross! After they have conquered, they will sit with Christ on his throne. This matches the sighting of the multitudes from all nations who were found at the throne of God:

> After this I looked, and behold, a great multitude that no one could number, from every nation, from all tribes and peoples and languages, standing before the throne and before the Lamb, clothed in white robes, with palm branches in their hands, ¹⁰ and crying out with a loud voice, "Salvation belongs to our God who sits on the throne, and to the Lamb!" (Rev 7:9-10)

3

The Precursors: Emergence of the Four Horsemen

3.1. INSIGHT INTO THE COURT OF GOD

After this I looked, and behold, a door standing open in heaven! And the first voice, which I had heard speaking to me like a trumpet, said, "Come up here, and I will show you what must take place after this." ² At once I was in the Spirit, and behold, a throne stood in heaven, with one seated on the throne. ³ And he who sat there had the appearance of jasper and carnelian, and around the throne was a rainbow that had the appearance of an emerald. ⁴ Around the throne were twenty-four thrones, and seated on the thrones were twenty-four elders, clothed in white garments, with golden crowns on their heads. ⁵ From the throne came flashes of lightning, and rumblings and peals of thunder, and before the throne were burning seven torches of fire, which are the seven spirits of God, ⁶ and before the throne there was as it were a sea of glass, like crystal.

And around the throne, on each side of the throne, are four living creatures, full of eyes in front and behind: ⁷ the first living creature like a lion, the second living creature like an ox, the third living creature with the face of a man, and the fourth living creature like an eagle in flight. ⁸ And the four living creatures, each of them with six wings, are full of eyes all around and within, and day and night they never cease to say,

THE PRECURSORS: EMERGENCE OF THE FOUR HORSEMEN

> "Holy, holy, holy, is the Lord God Almighty, who was and is and is to come!"
> ⁹ And whenever the living creatures give glory and honor and thanks to him who is seated on the throne, who lives forever and ever, ¹⁰ the twenty-four elders fall down before him who is seated on the throne and worship him who lives forever and ever. They cast their crowns before the throne, saying,
> ¹¹ "Worthy are you, our Lord and God, to receive glory and honor and power, for you created all things, and by your will they existed and were created." (Rev 4:1–11)

Chapter 4 of the book of Revelation provides a rare insight on certain activities around the throne of God, as well as on some aspects of God's divine council referred to in Ps 82:

> God has taken his place in the divine council; in the midst of the gods he holds judgment. (Ps 82:1 1)

From this rare peek into the inner court (throne room) of God and from events revealed in other chapters of the book of Revelation, we could glean a lot of information on the magnificence and modus operandi around the throne of God. This chapter narrates a solemn event taking place in heaven, with great import to our world. There was a heavenly gathering, and the cynosure of the gathering is God sitting on a throne:

> A throne stood in heaven, with one seated on the throne. ³ And he who sat there had the appearance of jasper and carnelian. (Rev 4:2–3)

Perhaps this was the same throne Isaiah saw God seated upon:

> In the year that King Uzziah died I saw also the Lord sitting upon a throne, high and lifted up, and his train filled the temple. ² Above it stood the seraphims: each one had six wings; with twain he covered his face, and with twain he covered his feet, and with twain he did fly. ³ And one cried unto another, and said, Holy, holy, holy, is the Lord of hosts: the whole earth is full of his glory. (Isa 6:1–3 AV)

Seated around this throne that God sat on are twenty-four beings whom St. John refers to as elders. This description of the beings as elders might be a reflection of the fact that these beings have human resemblance but look quite old. Hence, it seems they are ancient/eternal beings and not of human origin. Significantly, these twenty-four beings also sit on thrones and have golden crowns on their heads:

> Around the throne were twenty-four thrones, and seated on the thrones were twenty-four elders, clothed in white garments, with golden crowns on their heads. (Rev 4:4)

This implies that they might be kings/rulers in charge of certain aspects of God's creation—perhaps of different planets, etc. From the setting presented, it becomes immediately clear who is in charge of this gathering. God, sitting on his throne at the center, with power, glory, and splendor exuding from his throne in the form of lightening, rumblings, and thunder, is clearly in charge. The twenty-four elders are members of his divine council/cabinet:

> From the throne came flashes of lightning, and rumblings and peals of thunder, and before the throne were burning seven torches of fire, which are the seven spirits of God, [6] and before the throne there was as it were a sea of glass, like crystal. (Rev 4:5)

Despite their apparent high-ranking positions signified by their sitting on thrones and with crowns on their heads (suggesting kingship), the twenty-four beings do not forget their place. They recognize God as the supreme who created everything:

> And whenever the living creatures give glory and honor and thanks to him who is seated on the throne, who lives forever and ever, [10] the twenty-four elders fall down before him who is seated on the throne and worship him who lives forever and ever. They cast their crowns before the throne, saying,
> [11] "Worthy are you, our Lord and God, to receive glory and honor and power, for you created all things, and by your will they existed and were created." (Rev 4:9–11)

The throne seems to be on a four-sided platform, because God's bodyguards (the four beings) are standing on each side around the throne:

> And around the throne, on each side of the throne, are four living creatures, full of eyes in front and behind: [7] the first living creature like a lion, the second living creature like an ox, the third living creature with the face of a man, and the fourth living creature like an eagle in flight. [8] And the four living creatures, each of them with six wings, are full of eyes all around and within, and day and night they never cease to say,
> "Holy, holy, holy, is the Lord God Almighty,
> who was and is and is to come!" (Rev 4:6–8)

3.1.1. The "Four Living Creatures"—Cherubim or Seraphim?

Cherubim and seraphim are prominent among heavenly beings who have been encountered by humans and recorded in the Bible. Although only glimpses of the heavenly creatures have been provided in different parts of the Bible, the seraphim and cherubim appear to have some common features, with slight differences.

The heavenly beings described by St. John as "four living creatures" in Rev 4 are similar to those Ezekiel saw in his vision (see box 3.1), with a few key differences such as six wings (John's vision) instead of four wings (Ezekiel's vision), and single faces (John's vision) instead of four faces (Ezekiel's vision). Hence, it is very likely that the four living creatures John saw were the seraphim that Isaiah saw (Isa 6:2) instead of the cherubim that Ezekiel saw, because they have six wings and one face each. Although Isaiah did not describe their faces as they were covered with wings, John saw the faces and was able to describe what they looked like. From John's and Isaiah's visions, it seems the seraphim perform the following key functions around the throne of God:

- perpetual praise and worship of God ("Holy, holy, holy, is the Lord God Almighty, who was and is and is to come!")
- Protecting God's throne ("And around the throne, on each side of the throne, are four living creatures")
- Communicating God's command/intentions (Now I watched when the Lamb opened one of the seven seals, and I heard one of the four living creatures say with a voice like thunder, "Come!" [Rev 6:1])

The cherubim featured prominently in Ezekiel's vision of God. Ezekiel initially referred to them as living creatures. This may be because previous mentions of cherubim in the Bible had been of inanimate objects made by Moses (the cherubs modeled in the ark of the covenant) and those in the temple of Solomon (1 Kgs 8:7).

Ezekiel later identified these living creatures as cherubim:

> And everyone had four faces: the first face was the face of the cherub, and the second face was a human face, and the third the face of a lion, and the fourth the face of an eagle. [15] And the cherubim mounted up. These were the living creatures that I saw by the Chebar canal. (Ezek 10:14-15)

It is instructive to note that in Ezek 1, one of the faces is described as the face of an ox; however, in Ezek 10, that face is described as the face of a cherub:

> As for the likeness of their faces, each had a human face. The four had the face of a lion on the right side, the four had the *face of an ox* on the left side, and the four had the face of an eagle. (Ezek 1:10)

> And everyone had four faces: the first face was the *face of the cherub,* and the second face was a human face, and the third the face of a lion, and the fourth the face of an eagle. (Ezek 10:14)

This may imply that a cherub naturally has a face like an ox. The primary function of seraphim and cherubim from John's vision (Revelation) and Ezekiel's vision appears to be protecting God (guardian). Hence, they are always found wherever God is. However, it seems the seraphim are in charge of protecting God when he is on his throne in heaven (Isa 6, Rev 4), and the cherubim are in charge of his protection when he is on the move or outside his heavenly throne (Ezekiel). A spiritual being referred to as the king of Tyre in Ezek 28 (this being could be Satan or the fallen being referred to as the Day Star, son of Dawn—Lucifer) is described in Ezekiel as a guardian cherub, which implies he must have been among the top bodyguards of God:

> You were an anointed *guardian* cherub. I placed you; you were on the holy mountain of God. (Ezek 28:14)

Box 3.1. Ezekiel's Vision of God and Cherubim

> And I looked, and, behold, a whirlwind came out of the north, a great cloud, and a fire infolding itself, and a brightness was about it, and out of the midst thereof as the colour of amber, out of the midst of the fire.[5] Also out of the midst thereof came the likeness of four living creatures. And this was their appearance; they had the likeness of a man.[6] And every one had four faces, and every one had four wings.[7] And their feet were straight feet; and the sole of their feet was like the sole of a calf's foot: and they sparkled like the colour of burnished brass.[8] And they had the hands of a man under their wings on their four sides; and they four had their faces and their wings.[9] Their wings were joined one to another; they turned not when they went; they went every one straight forward.[10] As for the likeness of their

faces, they four had the face of a man, and the face of a lion, on the right side: and they four had the face of an ox on the left side; they four also had the face of an eagle.[11] Thus were their faces: and their wings were stretched upward; two wings of every one were joined one to another, and two covered their bodies.[12] And they went every one straight forward: whither the spirit was to go, they went; and they turned not when they went.[13] As for the likeness of the living creatures, their appearance was like burning coals of fire, and like the appearance of lamps: it went up and down among the living creatures; and the fire was bright, and out of the fire went forth lightning.

[14] And the living creatures ran and returned as the appearance of a flash of lightning.[15] Now as I beheld the living creatures, behold one wheel upon the earth by the living creatures, with his four faces.[16] The appearance of the wheels and their work was like unto the colour of a beryl: and they four had one likeness: and their appearance and their work was as it were a wheel in the middle of a wheel.[17] When they went, they went upon their four sides: and they turned not when they went.[18] As for their rings, they were so high that they were dreadful; and their rings were full of eyes round about them four.[19] And when the living creatures went, the wheels went by them: and when the living creatures were lifted up from the earth, the wheels were lifted up.[20] Whithersoever the spirit was to go, they went, thither was their spirit to go; and the wheels were lifted up over against them: for the spirit of the living creature was in the wheels.[21] When those went, these went; and when those stood, these stood; and when those were lifted up from the earth, the wheels were lifted up over against them: for the spirit of the living creature was in the wheels.[22] And the likeness of the firmament upon the heads of the living creature was as the colour of the terrible crystal, stretched forth over their heads above.[23] And under the firmament were their wings straight, the one toward the other: everyone had two, which covered on this side, and everyone had two, which covered on that side, their bodies.

[24] And when they went, I heard the noise of their wings, like the noise of great waters, as the voice of the Almighty, the voice of speech, as the noise of an host: when they stood, they let down their wings.[25] And there was a voice from the firmament that was over their heads, when they stood, and had let down their wings.[26] And above the firmament that was over their heads was the likeness of a throne, as the appearance of a sapphire stone: and upon the likeness of the throne was the likeness as the appearance of a man above upon it.[27] And I saw as the

> colour of amber, as the appearance of fire round about within it, from the appearance of his loins even upward, and from the appearance of his loins even downward, I saw as it were the appearance of fire, and it had brightness round about.[28] As the appearance of the bow that is in the cloud in the day of rain, so was the appearance of the brightness round about. This was the appearance of the likeness of the glory of the Lord. And when I saw it, I fell upon my face, and I heard a voice of one that spake. (Ezek 1:4–28 AV)

3.2. AUTHORITY TO OPEN THE SEALS

Then I saw in the right hand of him who was seated on the throne a scroll written within and on the back, sealed with seven seals. [2] And I saw a mighty angel proclaiming with a loud voice, "Who is worthy to open the scroll and break its seals?" [3] And no one in heaven or on earth or under the earth was able to open the scroll or to look into it, [4] and I began to weep loudly because no one was found worthy to open the scroll or to look into it. [5] And one of the elders said to me, "Weep no more; behold, the Lion of the tribe of Judah, the Root of David, has conquered, so that he can open the scroll and its seven seals."

[6] And between the throne and the four living creatures and among the elders I saw a Lamb standing, as though it had been slain, with seven horns and with seven eyes, which are the seven spirits of God sent out into all the earth. [7] And he went and took the scroll from the right hand of him who was seated on the throne. [8] And when he had taken the scroll, the four living creatures and the twenty-four elders fell down before the Lamb, each holding a harp, and golden bowls full of incense, which are the prayers of the saints. [9] And they sang a new song, saying,

"Worthy are you to take the scroll and to open its seals, for you were slain, and by your blood you ransomed people for God from every tribe and language and people and nation,

[10] and you have made them a kingdom and priests to our God, and they shall reign on the earth."

[11] Then I looked, and I heard around the throne and the living creatures and the elders the voice of many angels, numbering myriads of myriads and thousands of thousands, [12] saying with a loud voice,

"Worthy is the Lamb who was slain,
　to receive power and wealth and wisdom and might

THE PRECURSORS: EMERGENCE OF THE FOUR HORSEMEN   43

and honor and glory and blessing!"

[13] And I heard every creature in heaven and on earth and under the earth and in the sea, and all that is in them, saying,

"To him who sits on the throne and to the Lamb be blessing and honor and glory and might forever and ever!"

[14] And the four living creatures said, "Amen!" and the elders fell down and worshiped. (Rev 5:1–14)

Chapter 5 of the book of Revelation centers on John's vision of a key event in heaven where the end-time plans of God, contained in a scroll sealed with seven seals, are handed over to Jesus Christ. This scroll is so important and highly classified that no one in heaven, on earth, or under the earth has the authority to open it except Jesus Christ, presented in this vision as the "Lamb who was slain" and "the Lion of the tribe of Judah, the Root of David [that] has conquered" (to clearly show the legal credentials that enable him to receive this authority to break the seals and open the scroll):

> And one of the elders said to me, "Weep no more; behold, the Lion of the tribe of Judah, the Root of David, has conquered, so that he can open the scroll and its seven seals." (Rev 5:5)

This authority was bestowed on Jesus Christ after he conquered Satan by his death on the cross and retrieved the authority and dominion over earth, which Satan had hitherto got by making Adam to fall. It makes absolute sense that since the events were for the earth and its inhabitants, only the heavenly representative of planet Earth in the divine council could this mystery be revealed to:

> Worthy are you to take the scroll and to open its seals, for you were slain, and by your blood you ransomed people for God from every tribe and language and people and nation, and you have made them a kingdom and priests to our God and they shall reign on the earth. (Rev 5:10).

Since it is only Jesus Christ who is authorized to take the scroll and open the seal, it makes sense that only he has the authority to reveal its contents to his church. This is very important, as it immediately sets out that the message is authentic, and people should pay serious attention to it. No other message can trump it.

Another important thing that jumps out of this passage is that the gathering is not an inner caucus meeting of the divine council. There are also numerous angels in attendance:

> Then I looked, and I heard around the throne and the living creatures and the elders the voice of many angels, numbering myriads of myriads and thousands of thousands. (Rev 5:11)

This setting matches the heavenly assembly described in Daniel's vision:

> As I looked, thrones were placed, and the Ancient of Days took his seat; his clothing was white as snow, and the hair of his head like pure wool; his throne was fiery flames; its wheels were burning fire. [10] A stream of fire issued and came out from before him; a thousand thousands served him, and ten thousand times ten thousand stood before him; the court sat in judgment, and the books were opened. (Dan 7:9-10)

3.2.1. The Command—God in Control of the Times

One thing that becomes clear as one goes through the book of Revelation is that God is in charge of the entirety of eschatological events. Only he will decide when the events will commence, as he is the one holding the scroll containing the blueprint of the events. It is only when he convenes that assembly (witnessed by John) that the scroll will be handed over to Jesus Christ to unseal. From this point, Jesus Christ takes charge of the operations, as it is only when he opens a seal that the event for that period commences. The commands for the riders of the four horses to emerge is issued by one of the seraphim around the throne, at the behest of Christ opening the seals.

3.3. THE MYSTERIES OF THE SEVEN SEALS

> Now I watched when the Lamb opened one of the seven seals, and I heard one of the four living creatures say with a voice like thunder, "Come!" [2] And I looked, and behold, a white horse! And its rider had a bow, and a crown was given to him, and he came out conquering, and to conquer. (Rev 6:1-2)

According to the book of Revelation, eschatological events will commence with the opening of the seals. Revelation 6 presents a summarized sequence of key events that will occur during this period. Confusion in interpreting the hidden mysteries of the book of Revelation usually starts from this chapter. The events are presented in a convoluted way, where the seals open up further events and, if not read and interpreted systematically, lead to misunderstanding. However, the chapter also holds the key and foundation of how to go about interpreting and understanding the key messages, which Jesus Christ wanted us to grasp.

At the breaking of each of the first four seals, a command goes forth from the throne of God to activate the chief actor prepared for the event:

> Now I watched when the Lamb opened one of the seven seals, and I heard one of the four living creatures say with a voice like thunder, "Come!" (Rev 6:1)

It is apparent from the description of the event that these actors are not of heavenly origin. They seem to be coming from a different realm, outside from where the command is being issued:

> And I looked, and behold, a white horse! (Rev 6:2)

They have been prepared and were only waiting for the command of God, to emerge. This buttresses the point that God holds the key to eschatological events—it is only when he is ready that the events shall commence. Although personalized as riders of different colored horses, these riders might as well be events instead of individuals as has previously been construed. It may also be both (double meaning)—such as the spiritual being driving the event.

3.4 THE FIRST SEAL—EMERGENCE OF THE WHITE HORSE RIDER

> Now I watched when the Lamb opened one of the seven seals, and I heard one of the four living creatures say with a voice like thunder, "Come!" [2] And I looked, and behold, a white horse! And its rider had a bow, and a crown was given to him, and he came out conquering, and to conquer. (Rev 6:1–2)

At the breaking of the first seal, one of the living creatures guarding the throne of God gives the command for the actor to appear on the scene. Three key elements are presented in this verse to help the reader to understand the character of this actor/rider: white horse, bow, and crown.

Normally, white signifies peace/holiness, and the white horse, on the face of it, seems to depict something peaceful/holy or perhaps innocuous. However, the rider/event is a deceptive character, who though not holy would appear as holy (or pretend to be peaceful). The bow without an arrow also buttresses this deception; the rider, even though ready for battle, does not want to be seen as dangerous. "He came out conquering and to conquer" demonstrates how dangerous he is. This scene and character tend to warn of the surreptitious emergence of the antichrist or establishment of antichrist system. This white rider is a subterfuge that will mark the beginning of the end-time events. However, this event may largely go unnoticed. He will appear on the eschatology scene without raising much concern, while still achieving his goal of conquering the world.

It is interesting to note that Jesus Christ starts his description of the end-time events by warning Christians not to fall for deceptions:

> "Watch out that no one deceives you. For many will come in my name, claiming, 'I am the Messiah,' and will deceive many." (Matt 24:4–5 NIV)

This suggests that the initial event that will mark the beginning of the end-time is the rising of the antichrist, who will come with deceptive actions that will enable him to conquer nations without being noticed. Daniel described the antichrist as the little horn, signifying that the antichrist will largely be inconspicuous when he emerges onto the world stage:

> I considered the horns, and behold, there came up among them another horn, a little one, before which three of the first horns were plucked up by the roots. And behold, in this horn were eyes like the eyes of a man, and a mouth speaking great things. (Dan 7:8)

The little horn is also mentioned in Dan 8:

> Out of one of them came a little horn, which grew exceedingly great toward the south, toward the east, and toward the glorious land. [10] It grew great, even to the host of heaven. And some of the host and some of the stars it threw down to the ground and trampled on them. [11] It became great, even as great as the Prince of the host. And the regular burnt offering was taken away from him, and the place of his sanctuary was overthrown. (Dan 8:9–11)

His cunning and deceptive emergence is also mentioned by Daniel:

> And at the latter end of their kingdom, when the transgressors have reached their limit, a king of bold face, one who understands riddles, shall arise. [24] His power shall be great—but not by his own power; and he shall cause fearful destruction and shall succeed in what he does, and destroy mighty men and the people who are the saints. [25] By his cunning he shall make deceit

prosper under his hand, and in his own mind he shall become great. Without warning he shall destroy many. And he shall even rise up against the Prince of princes, and he shall be broken—but by no human hand. (Dan 8:23–25)

The second point is the fact that he emerges not as a king, but at some point, a crown is given him. So sometime after he emerges, a crown will be given to him before he starts to conquer ("*and a crown was given to him, and he came out conquering*"). This implies that whoever will be the antichrist will originally not have a crown (be a king/ruler with authority), but before he starts to fully operate, he will be made a king (giving authority of a king/ruler). This also aligns with Daniel's vision, where he described him as one who had no royal majesty but would obtain the kingdom via flattery and deceit:

In his place shall arise a contemptible person to whom royal majesty has not been given. He shall come in without warning and obtain the kingdom by flatteries. [22] Armies shall be utterly swept away before him and broken, even the prince of the covenant. [23] And from the time that an alliance is made with him he shall act deceitfully, and he shall become strong with a small people. [24] Without warning he shall come into the richest parts of the province, and he shall do what neither his fathers nor his fathers' fathers have done, scattering among them plunder, spoil, and goods. He shall devise plans against strongholds, but only for a time. (Dan 11:21–24)

3.5. THE SECOND SEAL—THE EMERGENCE OF THE RED HORSE (CHAOS AND WARS— END-TIME GEOPOLITICAL WARS)

When the Lamb opened the second seal, I heard the second living creature say, "Come!" Then another horse came out, a fiery red one. Its rider was given power to take peace from the earth and to make people kill each other. To him was given a large sword." (Rev 6:3–4)

This phase of the end-time will be marked by increased violence, chaos, and wars. The spiritual being behind this period will increase hatred and strife that will make people kill each other. This tallies with the events presented by Jesus Christ in the Gospels:

You will hear of wars and rumours of wars, but see to it that you are not alarmed. Such things must happen, but the end is still to come. ⁷ Nation will rise against nation, and kingdom against kingdom. (Matt 24:6–7)

In contrast to the events of the first seal, which may go largely unnoticed by the world, the second seal events will be very overt and observable by people, that any active watcher will recognize the arrival of the end-time period.

These wars of the second seal ("Nation will rise against nation, and kingdom against kingdom") referenced by Jesus Christ will largely be centered around the Near/Middle East (Arabian Peninsula, Egypt, Cyprus, Iraq, Iran, Jordan, Israel, Lebanon, Syria, Turkey, and Palestinian territory). Although it may also involve other countries around the world, such as NATO/Western countries rallying around Turkey and Israel, the initial key players will be Iran and Turkey. The key outcome of these wars will be the establishment of the antichrist kingdom/government (the beast system).

3.5.1. The Rise of the Beast System/Empire

Box 3.2. Daniel's Vision of a Ram and a Goat

> In the third year of King Belshazzar's reign, I, Daniel, had a vision, after the one that had already appeared to me. ² In my vision I saw myself in the citadel of Susa in the province of Elam; in the vision I was beside the Ulai Canal. ³ I looked up, and there before me was a ram with two horns, standing beside the canal, and the horns were long. One of the horns was longer than the other but grew up later. ⁴ I watched the ram as it charged toward the west and the north and the south. No animal could stand against it, and none could rescue from its power. It did as it pleased and became great.
>
> ⁵ As I was thinking about this, suddenly a goat with a prominent horn between its eyes came from the west, crossing the whole earth without touching the ground. ⁶ It came toward the two-horned ram I had seen standing beside the canal and charged at it in great rage. ⁷ I saw it attack the ram furiously, striking the ram and shattering its two horns. The ram was powerless to stand against it; the goat knocked it to the ground and trampled on it, and none could rescue the ram from its power. ⁸ The goat became very great, but at the height of its power

THE PRECURSORS: EMERGENCE OF THE FOUR HORSEMEN   49

the large horn was broken off, and in its place four prominent horns grew up toward the four winds of heaven.

⁹ Out of one of them came another horn, which started small but grew in power to the south and to the east and toward the Beautiful Land. ¹⁰ It grew until it reached the host of the heavens, and it threw some of the starry host down to the earth and trampled on them. ¹¹ It set itself up to be as great as the commander of the army of the Lord; it took away the daily sacrifice from the Lord, and his sanctuary was thrown down. ¹² Because of rebellion, the Lord's people and the daily sacrifice were given over to it. It prospered in everything it did, and truth was thrown to the ground.

¹³ Then I heard a holy one speaking, and another holy one said to him, "How long will it take for the vision to be fulfilled—the vision concerning the daily sacrifice, the rebellion that causes desolation, the surrender of the sanctuary and the trampling underfoot of the Lord's people?"

¹⁴ He said to me, "It will take 2,300 evenings and mornings; then the sanctuary will be reconsecrated."

The Interpretation of the Vision

¹⁵ While I, Daniel, was watching the vision and trying to understand it, there before me stood one who looked like a man. ¹⁶ And I heard a man's voice from the Ulai calling, "Gabriel, tell this man the meaning of the vision."

¹⁷ As he came near the place where I was standing, I was terrified and fell prostrate. "Son of man," he said to me, "understand that the vision concerns the time of the end."

¹⁸ While he was speaking to me, I was in a deep sleep, with my face to the ground. Then he touched me and raised me to my feet.

¹⁹ He said: "I am going to tell you what will happen later in the time of wrath, because the vision concerns the appointed time of the end. ²⁰ The two-horned ram that you saw represents the kings of Media and Persia. ²¹ The shaggy goat is the king of Greece, and the large horn between its eyes is the first king. ²² The four horns that replaced the one that was broken off represent four kingdoms that will emerge from his nation but will not have the same power.

²³ "In the latter part of their reign, when rebels have become completely wicked, a fierce-looking king, a master of intrigue, will arise. ²⁴ He will become very strong, but not by his own power. He will cause astounding devastation and will succeed in whatever he does. He will destroy those who are mighty, the

> holy people. ²⁵ He will cause deceit to prosper, and he will consider himself superior. When they feel secure, he will destroy many and take his stand against the Prince of princes. Yet he will be destroyed, but not by human power.
>
> ²⁶ "The vision of the evenings and mornings that has been given you is true, but seal up the vision, for it concerns the distant future."
>
> ²⁷ I, Daniel, was worn out. I lay exhausted for several days. Then I got up and went about the king's business. I was appalled by the vision; it was beyond understanding. (Dan 8:1–27 NIV)

Daniel 8 provides a lot of clues that could be used to understand how the beast/antichrist system of governance will be established. While in exile in Babylon, Daniel had a vision where things that would happen around the end-time were revealed to him. Although certain events that happened in the past (some closer to the time of Daniel) appear to be the fulfilment of this vision, the angel (Gabriel) who interpreted the vision to Daniel was very clear that the vision concerns things that would happen during the end-time. His interpretation started with this caveat:

> "Son of man," he said to me, "*understand that the vision concerns the time of the end.*" (Dan 8:17 NIV)

Judging from the interpretation of the vision, the ram with two horns is Iran:

> The two-horned ram that you saw represents the kings of Media and Persia. (Dan 8:20 NIV)

The reason is that present-day Iran is the remnant of the Medo-Persian Empire. Simply put, Iran is Persia, and its current map largely covers the area previous known as Persia and Medes. The two horns of the ram were described as the two kings of Media and Persia. This also perfectly fits present-day Iran, considering that Iran is essentially led by two leaders: the president and the supreme leader. The president is the head of government of the Islamic Republic of Iran but subject to the supreme leader. Whereas the president is the head of government, the supreme leader of Iran is the head of state and the highest political and religious authority of the Islamic Republic of Iran. Even though the supreme leader normally stays in the backstage (not usually facing the public), he controls key government establishments such as the armed forces, judiciary, state television, Guardian Council, and Expediency Discernment Council. According to the Iranian constitution of 1979, the powers of government in the country are vested in the legislature, the judiciary, and the executive powers, functioning under the supervision of the supreme leader. Hence, the president, alongside others, is subject to the supreme leader.

This present arrangement of governance in Iran where the supreme leader stays backstage is aptly captured by the description of the horns of the ram:

> I raised my eyes and saw, and behold, a ram standing on the bank of the canal. It had two horns, and both horns were high, but one was higher than the other, and the higher one came up last. (Dan 8:3)

The crux of the vision is that at a point towards the end-time, Iran (presented as the ram) will attempt to overrun other countries around it. As a matter of fact, the process of the establishment of the beast empire will commence at this point, when Iran began to attack/invade all countries around it (north, west, and south):

> I watched the ram as it charged toward the west and the north and the south. No animal could stand against it, and none could rescue from its power. It did as it pleased and became great. (Dan 8:4 NIV)

This move by the ram (Iran) will be countered by the goat coming from the west:

> As I was thinking about this, suddenly a goat with a prominent horn between its eyes came from the west, crossing the whole earth without touching the ground. ⁶ It came toward the two-horned ram I had seen standing beside the canal and charged at it in great rage. ⁷ I saw it attack the ram furiously, striking the ram and shattering its two horns. The ram was powerless to stand against it; the goat knocked it to the ground and trampled on it, and none could rescue the ram from its power. (Dan 8:5–7 NIV)

Remarkably, this goat has one horn (king), unlike the ram that has two horns. The horn is described as being conspicuous, thus this leader must be wielding tremendous power in his country. Judging from where Susa and the Ulai carnal is situated (Holman Bible Atlas, 1998, pp 165, plate 83), the following countries lie to the west: Iraq, Syria, Lebanon, Jordan, Israel, Turkey, Greece, and Cyprus.

Thus, the ram could be coming from any of these countries. The country was identified by the angel as Greece/Javan (depending on which Bible translation one chooses):

And the young he-goat, the hairy one, [is] the king of Javan; and the great horn that [is] between its eyes is the first king. (Dan 8:21 YLT)

And the goat is the king of Greece. And the great horn between his eyes is the first king. (Dan 8:21 ESV)

This is usually where many conclude that the vision was concerning the defeat of the Medo-Persian Empire (ram with two horns) by Alexander the Great (goat). However, Gabriel was very clear in his interpretation that the vision concerns things of the end-time: "understand that the vision concerns the time of the end" (Dan 8:17 NIV). Thus, the goat could not have been Alexander the Great. However, it does seem that the past events were foreshadows of what to expect during the end-time.

Although many Bible translations have the goat identified as Greece, others translate this as Javan, which is more encompassing. Javan is usually used to refer to islands and countries around the Aegean Sea. It essentially covers present-day Greece, the islands in the Aegean Sea, Anatolia (present-day Turkey), Cyprus, and Rhodes (see Box 3.3).

Box 3.3. Where Was Javan?

> Javan (Hebrew word for deceiver or one who makes sad) was a descendant of Noah (the fourth son of Japheth). He had four sons, namely: Elishah, associated with the Aegean nations; Tarshish, with Tarsus in Anatolia; Kittim, with Kition in modern Cyprus; and Dodanim, with the island of Rhodes.[10]

However, in the current dispensation, among all the countries in ancient Javan, Turkey seems to be the only one with the necessarily powers to withstand Iran. This conflict may possibly resolve into Shiite versus Sunni war. There is a high likelihood that Turkey will resurrect the Ottoman Empire. It is from this resurrected Ottoman Empire that the antichrist empire will emerge (see §6.4.8 for details). It may be that while this new Ottoman Empire is rising, Turkey will take over these other countries in the Javan area. It is no secret that the current president of Turkey is planning to rebuild the Ottoman Empire. Jonathan Gorvett, in an article in the *Asia Times* titled "Turkey's Vision of a Brave, New Ottoman Empire," has the following to say:

---

10. (https://amazingbibletimeline.com/blog/javan/#:~:text=He%20had%20four%20sons%2C%20namely%3B%20Elishah%20associated%20with,The%20Ionians%20dwelt%20in%20the%20land%20of%20Iona.)

President Recep Tayyip Erdogan's pro-Islamist government sees itself as heir to the Ottoman Empire, realm of the last Islamic Caliphate that controlled much of southeastern Europe from the 14th to early 20th century before being abolished in 1924.

Its perceived ambitions have been dubbed "neo-Ottomanism," a term laden with historical conquest that raises modern-day concerns about Ankara's intentions towards its smaller neighbors, including Greece, Cyprus and Libya, and broader regional vision.

By challenging treaties and boundaries that have existed in the region for nearly a century, Turkey's government hopes to secure a dominant position in the region. In doing so, it is also bringing an end to NATO and Western dominance to the geography, accelerating the birth of a new, multi-polar world—with all its associated uncertainties and risks.[11]

In September 2021, Cyprus's foreign minister accused Turkey's president of attempting to promote a new Ottoman Empire in the eastern Mediterranean and the Middle East: "What we are witnessing from Turkey is an attempt to promote a new Ottoman policy in the region. Turkey wants to become the regional hegemony," the Cypriot minister Nikos Christodoulides said in an interview with the Associated Press.[12]

Hence, it may be a case that when Iran (the ram) begins to attack and overrun countries in the Middle East, the new Ottoman Empire headed by Turkey will galvanize forces around the Middle East, possibly with Israel and Western countries joining hands to defeat Iran. The use of the phrase "is the first king" (Dan 8:21) to describe the horn of the goat might mean the first king/emperor of the renewed Ottoman Empire. This may or may not be the current president of Turkey, depending on when this will happen.

It is not far-fetched to see why Israel and other Western countries (under the aegis of NATO) could possibly join the Turkish Islamic/Sunni alliance to go against Iran. Turkey is a NATO member, and if it comes under attack, other NATO countries are obligated to rally round it, under NATO's Article 5 of the Washington Treaty (collective defence, where an attack against one ally is considered as an attack against all allies).

In addition, there is no love lost between Israel and Iran. As a matter of fact, Israel will be the prime target for any Iranian invasion of the Middle East. Hence, it makes sense that Israel will join forces that are against Iran. This inclusion of Israel in the alliance against Iran may be the premise on which the antichrist will establish a peace treaty with Israel (as they will

11. Gorvett, "Turkey's Vision."
12. Lederer, "Cyprus' Top Diplomat."

initially be on the same side in defeating Iran) that will last for a while, before he breaks it and invade Israel:

> And he shall make a strong covenant with many for one week, and for half of the week he shall put an end to sacrifice and offering. And on the wing of abominations shall come one who makes desolate, until the decreed end is poured out on the desolator. (Dan 9:27)

Following on from the vision, after the goat has defeated the ram, it grew in strength and power:

> Then the goat became exceedingly great, but when he was strong, the great horn was broken, and instead of it there came up four conspicuous horns toward the four winds of heaven. (Dan 8:8)

This king that defeated the ram will be killed or overthrown, and out of the empire he forged, four kings will emerge (see §3.5.1). It would make sense that once Iran has been defeated by the alliance Turkey helped to forge, other countries, such as Saudi Arabia, who may have been part of that alliance may want to pull out from the authoritarian regime of the new Ottoman Empire. This may lead to a conflict that will result in the demise of the first emperor and the division of the empire. These four kingdoms that will emerge are the four beasts mentioned in Dan 7:

> And four great beasts came up out of the sea, different from one another. [4] The first was like a lion and had eagles' wings. Then as I looked its wings were plucked off, and it was lifted up from the ground and made to stand on two feet like a man, and the mind of a man was given to it. [5] And behold, another beast, a second one, like a bear. It was raised up on one side. It had three ribs in its mouth between its teeth; and it was told, 'Arise, devour much flesh.' [6] After this I looked, and behold, another, like a leopard, with four wings of a bird on its back. And the beast had four heads, and dominion was given to it. [7] After this I saw in the night visions, and behold, a fourth beast, terrifying and dreadful and exceedingly strong. It had great iron teeth; it devoured and broke in pieces and stamped what was left with its feet. It was different from all the beasts that were before it, and it had ten horns. [8] I considered the horns, and behold, there came up among them another horn, a little one, before which three of the first horns were plucked up by the roots. And behold, in this horn were eyes like the eyes of a man, and a mouth speaking great things. (Dan 7:3–8)

THE PRECURSORS: EMERGENCE OF THE FOUR HORSEMEN

Importantly, the antichrist will emerge in the scene after the demise/breakup of the empire/kingdom into four parts (or emergence of four successive kingdoms) (see §3.5.2):

> Out of one of them came a little horn, which grew exceedingly great toward the south, toward the east, and toward the glorious land. [10] It grew great, even to the host of heaven. And some of the host and some of the stars it threw down to the ground and trampled on them. [11] It became great, even as great as the Prince of the host. And the regular burnt offering was taken away from him, and the place of his sanctuary was overthrown. [12] And a host will be given over to it together with the regular burnt offering because of transgression, and it will throw truth to the ground, and it will act and prosper. (Dan 8:8–12)

This also matches with the vision presented in Revelation concerning the beast system. Considering the beast of Rev 17 with seven heads (§6.4.8), the sixth empire will stem from the remnant of the fifth—i.e., Turkey, which is part of the old Ottoman Empire, will reestablish the sixth kingdom (new Ottoman Empire). Subsequently, this empire will be broken into four parts, which becomes the second dispensation of the new Ottoman Empire (the seventh head). From this seventh head, the antichrist empire will emerge:

> This calls for a mind with wisdom: the seven heads are seven mountains on which the woman is seated; [10] they are also seven kings, five of whom have fallen, one is, the other has not yet come, and when he does come he must remain only a little while. [11] As for the beast that was and is not, it is an eighth but it belongs to the seven, and it goes to destruction. (Rev 17:9–10)

The entire event narrated here is key to knowing when the end-time period has commenced. It is a prominent precursor event that will definitely point to the emergence of the end-time. Put simply, anytime you see Iran launching a full-scale invasion of countries around it, especially those in the Middle East, and Turkey or any other country west of Iran rallies multinational forces to go against it, know that the time has arrived!

3.5.2. End-Time Geopolitical Wars

> Nation will rise against nation, and kingdom against kingdom. (Matt 24:7)

And as for me, in the first year of Darius the Mede, I stood up to confirm and strengthen him.² And now I will show you the truth. Behold, three more kings shall arise in Persia, and a fourth shall be far richer than all of them. And when he has become strong through his riches, he shall stir up all against the kingdom of Greece. ³ Then a mighty king shall arise, who shall rule with great dominion and do as he wills. ⁴ And as soon as he has arisen, his kingdom shall be broken and divided toward the four winds of heaven, but not to his posterity, nor according to the authority with which he ruled, for his kingdom shall be plucked up and go to others besides these.

⁵ Then the king of the south shall be strong, but one of his princes shall be stronger than he and shall rule, and his authority shall be a great authority. ⁶ After some years they shall make an alliance, and the daughter of the king of the south shall come to the king of the north to make an agreement. But she shall not retain the strength of her arm, and he and his arm shall not endure, but she shall be given up, and her attendants, he who fathered her, and he who supported her in those times.

⁷ And from a branch from her roots one shall arise in his place. He shall come against the army and enter the fortress of the king of the north, and he shall deal with them and shall prevail. ⁸ He shall also carry off to Egypt their gods with their metal images and their precious vessels of silver and gold, and for some years he shall refrain from attacking the king of the north. ⁹ Then the latter shall come into the realm of the king of the south but shall return to his own land.

¹⁰ His sons shall wage war and assemble a multitude of great forces, which shall keep coming and overflow and pass through, and again shall carry the war as far as his fortress. ¹¹ Then the king of the south, moved with rage, shall come out and fight against the king of the north. And he shall raise a great multitude, but it shall be given into his hand. ¹² And when the multitude is taken away, his heart shall be exalted, and he shall cast down tens of thousands, but he shall not prevail. ¹³ For the king of the north shall again raise a multitude, greater than the first. And after some years he shall come on with a great army and abundant supplies.

¹⁴ In those times many shall rise against the king of the south, and the violent among your own people shall lift themselves up in order to fulfill the vision, but they shall fail. ¹⁵ Then the king of the north shall come and throw up siegeworks and take a well-fortified city. And the forces of the south shall not stand, or even his best troops, for there shall be no strength

to stand. [16] But he who comes against him shall do as he wills, and none shall stand before him. And he shall stand in the glorious land, with destruction in his hand. [17] He shall set his face to come with the strength of his whole kingdom, and he shall bring terms of an agreement and perform them. He shall give him the daughter of women to destroy the kingdom, but it shall not stand or be to his advantage. [18] Afterward he shall turn his face to the coastlands and shall capture many of them, but a commander shall put an end to his insolence. Indeed, he shall turn his insolence back upon him. [19] Then he shall turn his face back toward the fortresses of his own land, but he shall stumble and fall, and shall not be found.

[20] Then shall arise in his place one who shall send an exactor of tribute for the glory of the kingdom. But within a few days he shall be broken, neither in anger nor in battle. [21] In his place shall arise a contemptible person to whom royal majesty has not been given. He shall come in without warning and obtain the kingdom by flatteries. [22] Armies shall be utterly swept away before him and broken, even the prince of the covenant. [23] And from the time that an alliance is made with him he shall act deceitfully, and he shall become strong with a small people. [24] Without warning he shall come into the richest parts of the province, and he shall do what neither his fathers nor his fathers' fathers have done, scattering among them plunder, spoil, and goods. He shall devise plans against strongholds, but only for a time. [25] And he shall stir up his power and his heart against the king of the south with a great army. And the king of the south shall wage war with an exceedingly great and mighty army, but he shall not stand, for plots shall be devised against him. [26] Even those who eat his food shall break him. His army shall be swept away, and many shall fall down slain. [27] And as for the two kings, their hearts shall be bent on doing evil. They shall speak lies at the same table, but to no avail, for the end is yet to be at the time appointed. [28] And he shall return to his land with great wealth, but his heart shall be set against the holy covenant. And he shall work his will and return to his own land.

[29] At the time appointed he shall return and come into the south, but it shall not be this time as it was before. [30] For ships of Kittim shall come against him, and he shall be afraid and withdraw, and shall turn back and be enraged and take action against the holy covenant. He shall turn back and pay attention to those who forsake the holy covenant. [31] Forces from him shall appear and profane the temple and fortress, and shall take away the regular burnt offering. And they shall set up the abomination

that makes desolate. ³² He shall seduce with flattery those who violate the covenant, but the people who know their God shall stand firm and take action. ³³ And the wise among the people shall make many understand, though for some days they shall stumble by sword and flame, by captivity and plunder. ³⁴ When they stumble, they shall receive a little help. And many shall join themselves to them with flattery, ³⁵ and some of the wise shall stumble, so that they may be refined, purified, and made white, until the time of the end, for it still awaits the appointed time.

³⁶ And the king shall do as he wills. He shall exalt himself and magnify himself above every god, and shall speak astonishing things against the God of gods. He shall prosper till the indignation is accomplished; for what is decreed shall be done. ³⁷ He shall pay no attention to the gods of his fathers, or to the one beloved by women. He shall not pay attention to any other god, for he shall magnify himself above all. ³⁸ He shall honor the god of fortresses instead of these. A god whom his fathers did not know he shall honor with gold and silver, with precious stones and costly gifts. ³⁹ He shall deal with the strongest fortresses with the help of a foreign god. Those who acknowledge him he shall load with honor. He shall make them rulers over many and shall divide the land for a price.

⁴⁰ At the time of the end, the king of the south shall attack him, but the king of the north shall rush upon him like a whirlwind, with chariots and horsemen, and with many ships. And he shall come into countries and shall overflow and pass through. ⁴¹ He shall come into the glorious land. And tens of thousands shall fall, but these shall be delivered out of his hand: Edom and Moab and the main part of the Ammonites. ⁴² He shall stretch out his hand against the countries, and the land of Egypt shall not escape. ⁴³ He shall become ruler of the treasures of gold and of silver, and all the precious things of Egypt, and the Libyans and the Cushites shall follow in his train. ⁴⁴ But news from the east and the north shall alarm him, and he shall go out with great fury to destroy and devote many to destruction. ⁴⁵ And he shall pitch his palatial tents between the sea and the glorious holy mountain. Yet he shall come to his end, with none to help him. (Dan 11:1–45)

Daniel 11 provides an insight into the geopolitical wars that will be raging in the Near East towards the end-time. These wars will orchestrate the surreptitious emergence of the antichrist into the world stage. These wars were succinctly and aptly captured by Christ as "nation against nation, kingdom against kingdom," because individual nations will eventually coalesce into

THE PRECURSORS: EMERGENCE OF THE FOUR HORSEMEN 59

unstable and delicate kingdoms/confederacies/empire, that may further break down.

The wars will eventually resolve into a series of conflicts between leaders of two predominant nations/empire referred to by Daniel as king of the South (headquartered in Egypt) and king of the North (Turkey or Syria). The antichrist will emerge from the northern kingdom and will eventually defeat the southern kingdom. The final empire will be galvanized by the antichrist, which it will use to go against Jesus Christ and the armies of heaven at the battle of Armageddon (see §6.6.2).

3.5.3. The Emergence of the Four Sub-Kingdoms

In the first year of Belshazzar king of Babylon, Daniel saw a dream and visions of his head as he lay in his bed. Then he wrote down the dream and told the sum of the matter. ² Daniel declared, "I saw in my vision by night, and behold, the four winds of heaven were stirring up the great sea. ³ And four great beasts came up out of the sea, different from one another. ⁴ The first was like a lion and had eagles' wings. Then as I looked its wings were plucked off, and it was lifted up from the ground and made to stand on two feet like a man, and the mind of a man was given to it. ⁵ And behold, another beast, a second one, like a bear. It was raised up on one side. It had three ribs in its mouth between its teeth; and it was told, 'Arise, devour much flesh.' ⁶ After this I looked, and behold, another, like a leopard, with four wings of a bird on its back. And the beast had four heads, and dominion was given to it. ⁷ After this I saw in the night visions, and behold, a fourth beast, terrifying and dreadful and exceedingly strong. It had great iron teeth; it devoured and broke in pieces and stamped what was left with its feet. It was different from all the beasts that were before it, and it had ten horns. ⁸ I considered the horns, and behold, there came up among them another horn, a little one, before which three of the first horns were plucked up by the roots. And behold, in this horn were eyes like the eyes of a man, and a mouth speaking great things.

⁹ "As I looked, thrones were placed, and the Ancient of Days took his seat;
   his clothing was white as snow,
      and the hair of his head like pure wool;
   his throne was fiery flames;

its wheels were burning fire.
¹⁰ A stream of fire issued
    and came out from before him;
a thousand thousands served him,
    and ten thousand times ten thousand stood before him;
the court sat in judgment,
    and the books were opened.

¹¹ "I looked then because of the sound of the great words that the horn was speaking. And as I looked, the beast was killed, and its body destroyed and given over to be burned with fire. ¹² As for the rest of the beasts, their dominion was taken away, but their lives were prolonged for a season and a time.

¹³ "I saw in the night visions, and behold, with the clouds of heaven there came one like a son of man, and he came to the Ancient of Days and was presented before him.

¹⁴ "And to him was given dominion and glory and a kingdom, that all peoples, nations, and languages should serve him; his dominion is an everlasting dominion, which shall not pass away, and his kingdom one that shall not be destroyed.

¹⁵ "As for me, Daniel, my spirit within me was anxious, and the visions of my head alarmed me. ¹⁶ I approached one of those who stood there and asked him the truth concerning all this. So he told me and made known to me the interpretation of the things. ¹⁷ 'These four great beasts are four kings who shall arise out of the earth. ¹⁸ But the saints of the Most High shall receive the kingdom and possess the kingdom forever, forever and ever.'

¹⁹ "Then I desired to know the truth about the fourth beast, which was different from all the rest, exceedingly terrifying, with its teeth of iron and claws of bronze, and which devoured and broke in pieces and stamped what was left with its feet, ²⁰ and about the ten horns that were on its head, and the other horn that came up and before which three of them fell, the horn that had eyes and a mouth that spoke great things, and that seemed greater than its companions. ²¹ As I looked, this horn made war with the saints and prevailed over them, ²² until the Ancient of Days came, and judgment was given for the saints of the Most High, and the time came when the saints possessed the kingdom.

²³ "Thus he said: 'As for the fourth beast, there shall be a fourth kingdom on earth, which shall be different from all the kingdoms, and it shall devour the whole earth, and trample it down, and break it to pieces. ²⁴ As for the ten horns, out of this kingdom ten kings shall arise, and another shall arise after them;

he shall be different from the former ones, and shall put down three kings.

²⁵ "'He shall speak words against the Most High, and shall wear out the saints of the Most High, and shall think to change the times and the law; and they shall be given into his hand for a time, times, and half a time. ²⁶ But the court shall sit in judgment, and his dominion shall be taken away, to be consumed and destroyed to the end.

²⁷ "'And the kingdom and the dominion and the greatness of the kingdoms under the whole heaven shall be given to the people of the saints of the Most High; his kingdom shall be an everlasting kingdom, and all dominions shall serve and obey him.'

²⁸ "Here is the end of the matter. As for me, Daniel, my thoughts greatly alarmed me, and my color changed, but I kept the matter in my heart." (Dan 7:1–28)

This portrays that the empire/confederation of nations formed by the goat (Turkey) that is the new Ottoman Empire will be split into four after the ram (Iran) has been defeated. The Turkish leader who orchestrated this empire will be killed in the process that will lead to the emergence of the four new kingdoms (the four beasts). From the fourth beast, the antichrist will emerge.

3.6. THE THIRD SEAL—EMERGENCE OF THE BLACK HORSE RIDER (FAMINE)

When the Lamb opened the third seal, I heard the third living creature say, "Come!" I looked, and there before me was a black horse! Its rider was holding a pair of scales in his hand. ⁶ Then I heard what sounded like a voice among the four living creatures, saying, "Two pounds of wheat for a day's wages, and six pounds of barley for a day's wages, and do not damage the oil and the wine!" (Rev 6:5–6)

This period of the end-time will be marked by economic collapse and increased hunger. Inflation will be so high that a day's wage will hardly afford anything tangible. It may be that the wars preceding this event may have disrupted the global agricultural sector and other economic activities that will affect the global economic market. The impact of wars on global economy and food availability is made clearer in view of the ongoing war between Russia and Ukraine. A major war involving many countries in the Near East would trigger a major disruption in global oil and gas supplies, which would cause havoc in the global supply chain. Christ hinted at this in the Gospels:

> There will be famines and earthquakes in various places. All these are the beginning of birth pains. (Matt 24:7–8)

An important point to note here is that Christians will still be in the world and will witness these events. This is the reason Christ cautioned that Christians should not be alarmed when these events start to unfold ("but see to it that you are not alarmed"). This contradicts the school of thought that believes that Christians will be removed or raptured before the birth pains and tribulation. Christ, by providing this caution, is asking Christians to brace themselves, as the current events/upheavals are merely birth pains compared to what is coming.

3.7. THE FOURTH SEAL—EMERGENCE OF THE PALE HORSE (PESTILENCE AND DEATH)

> When the Lamb opened the fourth seal, I heard the voice of the fourth living creature say, "Come!" [8] I looked, and there before me was a pale horse! Its rider was named Death, and Hades was following close behind him. They were given *power over a fourth of the earth to kill by sword, famine, and plague,* and by the wild beasts of the earth." (Rev 6:7–8)

This tallies with what God referred to in Ezek 14 as "four dreadful judgments":

> For this is what the Sovereign LORD says: How much worse will it be when I send against Jerusalem my four dreadful judgments—sword and famine and wild beasts and plague—to kill its men and their animals! (Ezek 14:21)

The same message is contained in Luke 21:

> There will be great earthquakes, and in various places *famines* and *pestilences*. And there will be terrors and great signs from heaven. (Luke 21:11)

Hence, at the end of the events of the fourth seal, one-quarter of the world's population will have died via war, economic collapse (famine), and pestilence (plagues/pandemic). At the present 7.8 billion population, it is expected that at least 1.9 billion people will have died at this point!

Interestingly, Christ made it clear that before these events, persecution of Christians will have heightened. However, Christians are expected to embrace it and take it as an opportunity to witness for God and perhaps gain more souls for Christ:

> But before all this they will lay their hands on you and persecute you, delivering you up to the synagogues and prisons, and you will be brought before kings and governors for my name's sake. This will be your opportunity to bear witness. (Luke 21:12–13)

3.8. THE ANTICHRIST'S PEACE DEAL (COVENANT) WITH ISRAEL

There are indications that when the antichrist is waging war against other countries in the Middle East, Israel will initially be spared, because it had signed a deal with the antichrist. Israel will falsely feel secure because of this deal, as hinted by Isaiah:

> Therefore hear the word of the LORD, you scoffers, who rule this people in Jerusalem! ^{15} Because you have said, "We have made a covenant with death, and with Sheol we have an agreement, when the overwhelming whip passes through it will not come to us, for we have made lies our refuge, and in falsehood we have taken shelter." (Isa 28:14–15)

This treaty was also mentioned in the book of Daniel:

> And he shall make a strong covenant with many for one week and for half of the week he shall put an end to sacrifice and offering. And on the wing of abominations shall come one who makes desolate, until the decreed end is poured out on the desolator." (Dan 9:27)

The "one-week" deal is commonly referred to as the seven-years covenant (one prophetic day equivalent to one year). It is expected that this covenant will pave the way for the building of the third temple in Jerusalem within the first half of this period, and daily sacrifices as prescribed in the Old Testament will resume. However, this treaty will be broken midway by the antichrist, and he will attack Israel with his army, to install himself as God in the temple:

> Then your covenant with death will be annulled, and your agreement with Sheol will not stand; when the overwhelming scourge passes through, you will be beaten down by it. (Isa 28:18)

It is important to note here that the rider of the pale horse (fourth seal) is named Death, and Hades (Sheol) follows him (see §3.7). Daniel also noted the breaking of the deal, which will make way for the setting up of the abomination of desolation:

> He shall turn back and pay attention to those who forsake the holy covenant. [31] Forces from him shall appear and profane the temple and fortress, and shall take away the regular burnt offering. And they shall set up the abomination that makes desolate. [32] He shall seduce with flattery those who violate the covenant, but the people who know their God shall stand firm and take action. (Dan 11:30–31)

It could be glimpsed here that by entering into covenant with the antichrist, Israel will forsake the holy covenant their forefathers had made with God. By the time the antichrist sets himself up as God in the temple, some Jews and Christians will recognize this and stand firm against the antichrist. Jesus Christ admonished his followers to watch out for this incident, as it will be a marker that will trigger the great tribulation:

> So when you see the abomination of desolation spoken of by the prophet Daniel, standing in the holy place (let the reader understand), [16] then let those who are in Judea flee to the mountains. [17] Let the one who is on the housetop not go down to take what is in his house, [18] and let the one who is in the field not turn back to take his cloak. [19] And alas for women who are pregnant and for those who are nursing infants in those days! [20] Pray that your flight may not be in winter or on a Sabbath. [21] For then there will be great tribulation, such as has not been from the beginning of the world until now, no, and never will be. [22] And if those days had not been cut short, no human being would be saved. But for the sake of the elect those days will be cut short. (Matt 24:15–22)

Saint Paul also hinted that this desolation (desecration of the temple) will happen before the coming of Christ:

> Let no one deceive you in any way. For that day will not come, unless the rebellion comes first, and the man of lawlessness is revealed, the son of destruction, [4] who opposes and exalts himself against every so-called god or object of worship, so that he takes his seat in the temple of God, proclaiming himself to be God. (2 Thess 2:3–4)

3.9. THE FIFTH SEAL—PERSECUTION OF SAINTS AND MARTYRS

> When he opened the fifth seal, I saw under the altar the souls of those who had been slain for the word of God and for the witness they had borne. [10] They cried out with a loud voice, "O Sovereign Lord, holy and true, how long before you will judge and avenge our blood on those who dwell on the earth?" [11] Then they were each given a white robe and told to rest a little longer, until the number of their fellow servants and their brothers should be complete, who were to be killed as they themselves had been. (Rev 6:9–11)

When the fifth seal is opened, John is shown the souls of martyrs who have been killed "for the word of God and for the witness they had borne." This implies that Christians will be brutally persecuted by the agents of the antichrist during the period leading up to the great tribulation. Just as Jesus Christ warned, Christians will heavily be persecuted for bearing witness for Christ. And this will last for a set time, when a certain number of Christians shall have been killed ("*until the number of their fellow servants and their brothers should be complete, who were to be killed as they themselves had been*"). Saint Paul in the book of Romans admonished believers to accept this moment and rejoice in it:

> And not only so, but let us also rejoice in our tribulations: knowing that tribulation worketh patience. (Rom 5:3)

3.10. THE FALLING AWAY (APOSTASY) IN THE CHRISTIAN CHURCH

> Then you will be handed over to be persecuted and put to death, and you will be hated by all nations because of me. [10] At that time many will turn away from the faith and will betray and hate each other, [11] and many false prophets will appear and deceive many people. [12] Because of the increase of wickedness, the love of most will grow cold, [13] but the one who stands firm to the end will be saved. [14] And this gospel of the kingdom will be preached in the whole world as a testimony to all nations, and then the end will come. (Matt 24:9–14).

The hardships and increasing persecutions of Christians that will be rampant during the end-time will cause many believers to abandon their faith in God and Jesus Christ and accept antichrist as god. This event is usually referred to as the falling away or great apostasy (*apostasia*). Several factors will possibly contribute to Christians falling away from the faith. Some of these factors will include:

- Targeted persecutions of Christians—denial of fundamental rights, imprisonment, and death

- Belief in false doctrines—this is already permeating the various Christian churches and will increase towards the end-time. Many Christians will accept wrong doctrines that will lead them astray from the truth.

- False prophets and prophecies—many Christians are being led astray by many false prophets. These false prophets will be purveyors of false doctrines (doctrines of demons) that will cause many Christians to stumble in faith. Prophetic teachings linked to prosperity gospels are currently sweeping across the world, and less attention is being paid to the gospel of salvation. Most of these false teachings are disguised as deep teachings of the things of God, which have not been previously revealed, while in truth they are "deep things of Satan" (Rev 2:24). Christ warned about this, that many will come in his name to deceive others. The phrase "coming in his name" covers both those who will be claiming to be preaching in the name of Jesus Christ, while dishing out false teachings, and those who will outrightly claim to be Christ. Some of these false teachers and prophets are already in the world, and this will intensify during the end-time, as warned by Christ and St. Paul:

    > Now the Spirit speaketh expressly, that in the latter times some shall depart from the faith, giving heed to seducing spirits, and doctrines of devils; [2] Speaking lies in hypocrisy; having their conscience seared with a hot iron; (1 Timothy 4: 1-2 AV).

- Unpreparedness of Christians to face end-time persecutions

Many Christians are relying on the rapture as an escape route out of the great tribulation. The rapture in this context is literally a translation of believers from the earth to heaven, just before the troubles of the great tribulation commence. However, Jesus Christ did not say anything about this sort of rapture, neither did the apostles preach it, nor was it captured in Daniel's prophecies of the end-time. Christ essentially promised resurrection of the dead and eternal life for believers.

The downside of this belief in rapture is that many who believed they would be taken out of the dangers of the great tribulation and straight to heaven will be highly disappointed when they confront the antichrist and his agents right here on earth. This disappointment could spur disillusionment among Christians, which could cause many to succumb and deny the faith.

Snippets from various passages in the Bible suggest that the great tribulation will be a very terrible time, with wicked demons and fallen angels running amok across the earth. Only a well-prepared Christian will be able to withstand the antics of the antichrist and his agents. This is the reason Christ forewarned his followers and harped on patience and endurance till the end. In addition to persecutions, deception will be rife, and those who are not well grounded in their faith will turn from it to worship the antichrist as their god. This set of apostate Christians will be diametrically opposed to the true faith to the extent that they will betray their previous brethren in Christ. Paul referred to the "falling away" as rebellion, to show how grievous and dangerous this will be for Christians:

> Now concerning the coming of our Lord Jesus Christ and our being gathered together to him, we ask you, brothers, [2] not to be quickly shaken in mind or alarmed, either by a spirit or a spoken word, or a letter seeming to be from us, to the effect that the day of the Lord has come. [3] Let no one deceive you in any way. For that day will not come, unless the rebellion comes first, and the man of lawlessness is revealed, the son of destruction, [4] who opposes and exalts himself against every so-called god or object of worship, so that he takes his seat in the temple of God, proclaiming himself to be God. [5] Do you not remember that when I was still with you I told you these things? [6] And you know what is restraining him now so that he may be revealed in his time. [7] For the mystery of lawlessness is already at work. Only he who now restrains it will do so until he is out of the way. [8] *And then the lawless one will be revealed, whom the Lord Jesus will kill with the breath of his mouth and bring to nothing by the appearance of his coming.* [9] The coming of the lawless one is by the activity of Satan with all power and false signs and wonders, [10] and with all wicked deception for those who are perishing, because they refused to love the truth and so be saved. [11] Therefore God sends them a strong delusion, so that they may believe what is false, [12] in order that all may be condemned who did not believe the truth but had pleasure in unrighteousness. (2 Thess 2:1–12)

4

The Great Tribulation

4.1. EVENTS OF THE SIXTH SEAL

> When he opened the sixth seal, I looked, and behold, there was a great earthquake, and the sun became black as sackcloth, the full moon became like blood, [13] and the stars of the sky fell to the earth as the fig tree sheds its winter fruit when shaken by a gale. [14] The sky vanished like a scroll that is being rolled up, and every mountain and island was removed from its place. [15] Then the kings of the earth and the great ones and the generals and the rich and the powerful, and everyone, slave and free, hid themselves in the caves and among the rocks of the mountains, [16] calling to the mountains and rocks, "Fall on us and hide us from the face of him who is seated on the throne, and from the wrath of the Lamb, [17] for the great day of their wrath has come, and who can stand?" (Rev 6:12–17)

The sixth seal is the climax of the wrath of Satan. There are multiple events that occur at the opening of the sixth seal. Whereas some appear to be happening concurrently, other events appear to be sequential (following others). This period marks the time that the antichrist will establish himself as God and persecution will increase. Key events of this period include:

- Earthquake
- Eclipse
- War in the second heaven

THE GREAT TRIBULATION 69

- Displacement of Satan and his angels from the second heaven
- Sealing of the 144 Jews
- Escape of some Christians into the wilderness
- Empowerment of the antichrist and false prophet by the fallen dragon
- Appearance of souls of multitudes of people in heaven

4.2. GREAT EARTHQUAKE AND ECLIPSE (THREE DAYS OF DARKNESS?)

> When he opened the sixth seal, I looked, and behold, there was a great earthquake, and *the sun became black as sackcloth, the full moon became like blood*, and the stars of the sky fell to the earth as the fig tree sheds its winter fruit when shaken by a gale. (Rev 6:12–13)

The occurrence of a great earthquake that will shake the world and an eclipse that will envelop the world will mark the beginning of the great tribulation. There are speculations that this eclipse or darkness will be similar to that experienced by the Egyptians just before the exodus (ninth plague):

> Then the Lord said to Moses, "Stretch out your hand toward heaven, that there may be darkness over the land of Egypt, a darkness to be felt." 22 So Moses stretched out his hand toward heaven, and there was pitch darkness in all the land of Egypt [for] three days. 23 They did not see one another, nor did anyone rise from his place for three days, but all the people of Israel had light where they lived. (Exod 10:21–23)

Moses was told only that there would be darkness, without any specific duration; however, the darkness lasted for three days. This has led many to believe that the darkness/eclipse hinted at here in Revelation may also last for three days, even though St. John does not specify how long this darkness will last.

The darkness hinted at here will coincide or be closely followed by the fall of Satan and rebellious beings (angels, principalities, etc), who will be displaced from the second heaven to earth:

> And the stars of the sky fell to the earth as the fig tree sheds its winter fruit when shaken by a gale. (Rev 6:13)

Hence, it will be a very chaotic and dangerous time, with the principalities running amok in fury, going after humans, some of whom they may oppress, possess, or kill.

In addition to the eclipse and darkness, the great earthquake will cause a lot of havoc to many critical infrastructures that could result in the breakdown of essential services. This earthquake could also cause tsunamis and flooding:

> And every mountain and island was removed from its place. (Rev 6:14)

Hence, this will be a frightening time, especially to those who may not have prepared for it.

Amos also mentioned a day when the land will tremble (earthquake) and darkness will cover the land:

> The Lord has sworn by the pride of Jacob: "Surely, I will never forget any of their deeds. ⁸ Shall not the land tremble on this account, and everyone mourn who dwells in it, and all of it rise like the Nile, and be tossed about and sink again, like the Nile of Egypt? ⁹ And on that day," declares the Lord God, "I will make the sun go down at noon and darken the earth in broad daylight (Amos 8:7–9)

Isaiah may have hinted at this in one of his prophecies where he encouraged the people to hide behind closed doors until these events have passed:

> Come, my people, enter your chambers, and shut your doors behind you; hide yourselves for a little while until the fury has passed by.
> ²¹ For behold, the Lord is coming out from his place to punish the inhabitants of the earth for their iniquity, and the earth will disclose the blood shed on it, and will no more cover its slain. (Isa 26:20–21)

4.3. SATAN THROWN DOWN TO EARTH—THE ANGELIC WAR IN THE SECOND HEAVEN

When he opened the sixth seal, I looked, and behold, there was a great earthquake, and the sun became black as sackcloth, the full moon became like blood, *and the stars of the sky fell to the*

> earth as the fig tree sheds its winter fruit when shaken by a gale. (Rev 6:12–13)

> For he has humbled the inhabitants of the height, the lofty city. He lays it low, lays it low to the ground, casts it to the dust. [6] The foot tramples it, the feet of the poor, the steps of the needy. (Isa 26:5–6)

> All the host of heaven shall rot away, and the skies roll up like a scroll. All their host shall fall, as leaves fall from the vine, like leaves falling from the fig tree. (Isa 34:4)

> Out of one of them came a little horn, which grew exceedingly great toward the south, toward the east, and toward the glorious land. [10] *It grew great, even to the host of heaven. And some of the host and some of the stars it threw down to the ground and trampled on them.* (Dan 8:9–10)

The event described in Rev 6:12–13 is a very important event that is usually glossed over by many. Many see this only from peripheral aspects—as mere signs signifying the coming of Christ. However, this marks the commencements of events that will eventually lead to the coming of Christ. This is the point the angels/armies of heaven are clearing the way for Him. The angels are literally clearing the second heaven of Satan and his angels who have been occupying it since the last angelic war in the first heaven, that led to Satan and his soldiers being ejected from where the throne of God is. It is important to point out here that there are several heavens (realms). However, they are broadly classified into three: first heaven, second heaven (the astral plane occupied by Satan and fallen angels; however, the holy angels and humans do have access to it, as it lies between the earth and the first heaven), and the third heaven (the earth).

At the end of the first angelic war, Satan and his angels occupied strategic locations in the second heaven in order to disrupt communication and transmission of God's messages to the people on earth. This was hinted at in the book of Daniel, where the prince of Persia (one of the principalities under Satan) was preventing the passage of Gabriel whom God had dispatched to deliver a crucial message to Daniel:

> Then he said to me, "Fear not, Daniel, for from the first day that you set your heart to understand and humbled yourself before your God, your words have been heard, and I have come because of your words. [13] The prince of the kingdom of Persia withstood me twenty-one days, but Michael, one of the chief

princes, came to help me, for I was left there with the kings of Persia, [14] and came to make you understand what is to happen to your people in the latter days. For the vision is for days yet to come." (Dan 10:12–14)

This is an instructive passage detailing not only how strong this principality is (*withstanding* Gabriel until reinforcement came through Michael) but also the workings in the second heaven; both God's and Satan's angels can operate in this realm. Such principalities are so powerful that they control territories. Gabriel was most likely detained there at the second heaven, because he told Daniel that "I was left there with the kings of Persia"—until Michael came to the rescue. This also suggests that the kings of Persia were under the control of this prince, because Gabriel was detained there with them (perhaps their spirits). It seems this sort of fight is rampant between God's angels and Satan's princes, because Gabriel told Daniel that he would return to the second heaven to finish the fight:

> Then he said, "Do you know why I have come to you? But now I will return to fight against the prince of Persia; and when I go out, behold, the prince of Greece will come. [21] But I will tell you what is inscribed in the book of truth: there is none who contends by my side against these except Michael, your prince. (Dan 10:20–21)

The chapter contains important details that also point to the fact that Satan has his princes (principalities) manning various regions of the world and disrupting God's will, hence the reason Christ urged us in the Lord's Prayer to pray for the will of God to be done on earth—"Thy will be done on earth as it is in heaven."

In view of the foregoing, it would be easy to understand that this realm has to be conquered before Christ comes to earth to finish the battle with the antichrist. That is why the Bible records that the stars (fallen angels) are falling from heaven to earth:

> And the stars of the sky fell to the earth as the fig tree sheds its winter fruit when shaken by a gale. (Rev 6:13)

This war in the second heaven is expounded in Rev 12, when the dragon is thrown down to earth by Michael:

> Now war arose in heaven, Michael and his angels fighting against the dragon. And the dragon and his angels fought back, [8] but he was defeated, and there was no longer any place for them in heaven. [9] And the great dragon was thrown down, that ancient

THE GREAT TRIBULATION

serpent, who is called the devil and Satan, the deceiver of the whole world—he was thrown down to the earth, and his angels were thrown down with him. [10] And I heard a loud voice in heaven, saying, "Now the salvation and the power and the kingdom of our God and the authority of his Christ have come, for the accuser of our brothers has been thrown down, who accuses them day and night before our God. [11] And they have conquered him by the blood of the Lamb and by the word of their testimony, for they loved not their lives even unto death. [12] Therefore, rejoice, O heavens and you who dwell in them! But woe to you, O earth and sea, for the devil has come down to you in great wrath, because he knows that his time is short!" (Rev 12:7–12).

However, this is where most readers of the book of Revelation get thrown off course. Most readers tend to think this is a flashback to the first angelic war in heaven, because the chief characters in the two events (Michael and his angels and Satan/the dragon and his angels) are similar. However, there are pointers here to indicate that this is a different event and not a flashback to a past event:

1. Chapter 1 of the book of Revelation clearly indicates that what is about to be described is events that will soon happen and not events that have already occurred. In view of this, every vision in the book of Revelation must be read and interpreted as yet-to-occur events.

2. The first war in heaven was not the only time Michael fought with Satan. Michael also fought Satan when he wanted to steal the body of Moses—"But when the archangel Michael, contending with the devil, was disputing about the body of Moses, he did not presume to pronounce a blasphemous judgment, but said, 'The Lord rebuke you.'" (Jude 1:9)

3. There was really no need to flash back to the first angelic war amidst the events of the end-time. And if read as a flashback, it doesn't really add anything to the sequence of end-time events. However, when viewed as a war that is going to happen alongside other events of the end-time, the true meaning and rationale behind it emerge. A third of the stars falling down to earth also tallies with the stars that fall from the sky at the opening of the sixth seal.

4. The setting of the first war in heaven was in the third heaven. The purpose was to remove Satan from the presence of God—"And he said to them, 'I saw Satan fall like lightning from heaven'" (Luke

10:18)—whereas the purpose of this second war is to force Satan out of the spiritual realm (the heavenlies) into the physical realm (earth). Remember, Satan as a cherub was like a bodyguard to God (possibly, the aide-de-camp—ADC—of God) who "covereth" (Ezek 28:14). The sole purpose of the first war in heaven was to remove Satan from the direct presence of God. In the book of Job, Satan was no longer an inhabitant of the third heaven—at least, he was no longer in direct contact with God. This shows that the first war had already occurred. He merely came to join the assembly of the sons of God, and the venue could have been anywhere in the heavenlies ("Now there was a day when the sons of God came to present themselves before the LORD, and Satan also came among them" [Job 1:6].). The following verse clearly illustrates that Satan was no longer in direct contact with God, as he needed to render account to where he had been and what he had been up to ("The LORD said to Satan, 'From where have you come?' Satan answered the LORD and said, 'From going to and fro on the earth, and from walking up and down on it'" [Job 1:7].). However, despite the fact that Satan had been thrown down from heaven as Jesus Christ alluded to (Luke 10:18), Satan still had some stronghold in the heavenly realms ("Put on the whole armor of God, that you may be able to stand against the schemes of the devil. For we do not wrestle against flesh and blood, but against the rulers, against the authorities, against the cosmic powers over this present darkness, against the spiritual forces of evil in the heavenly places" [Eph 6:11–12].). Hence, if this realm (*heavenly* places) that is occupied by rebellious entities is not the third heaven, it must then be the second heaven!

5. The first angelic battle may have happened before Adam and Eve were created or before the fall, because at the point Satan was tempting Eve, he had become the enemy of God. However, the angelic battle mentioned in Revelation happens just prior the coming of Christ and his angels on the earth.

6. The action of the dragon after he falls also points to this. He goes after the woman and her son ("And when the dragon saw that he had been thrown down to the earth, he pursued the woman who had given birth to the male child" [Rev 12:13].). The woman referred to in this passage is the church, and the male child represents the Christians (most likely the great multitude found in heaven), whom Satan wanted to destroy, but they escaped the eternal damnation Satan had planned for them and made it to heaven. This will be discussed in detail in §4.4. This cannot be a description of the previous war in heaven. To

make readers understand this, the battle of the dragon and the woman is presented in Rev 12:1-6, before the description of the fall of the dragon in Rev 12:7-17. This is a way to make the reader link these two events. However, instead of linking these two events presented in Rev 12, most readers perceive this as a flashback of the first war in heaven and the birth of Christ. To them, the struggle between the woman and the dragon is an allusion to how Herod wanted to kill the child Jesus after his birth and God took him away to Egypt for safety. Even though this seems plausible, however, in Rev 7, as soon as the dragon falls, he goes after the woman and child, whereas we know that thousands of years passed between the first war in heaven and the birth of Christ. Thus, Rev 12 is not referring to this first war in heaven and the birth of Christ. Rather, it is referring to the events of the end-time when Satan and his angels are displaced from their heavenly places in the second heaven and thrown down on earth by Michael and his angels. This battle continues on earth, when Satan is finally defeated by Christ's angels, bundled up, and thrown into prison (bottomless pit).

7. There are important details in the narration of the fight between the dragon and Michael (Rev 12:7-12) that clearly point to the fact that this is an event that happens after creation and the death of Christ, in heaven. It is generally accepted that the first war in heaven happened before Adam was created. But this particular war in heaven being referred to here obviously happens after the death of Christ. The pointers are contained in the proclamation of the loud voice from heaven:

> Now the salvation and the power and the kingdom of our God and the authority of his Christ have come, for the accuser of our brothers has been thrown down, who accuses them day and night before our God. [11] And they have conquered him by the blood of the Lamb and by the word of their testimony, for they loved not their lives even unto death. [12] Therefore, rejoice, O heavens and you who dwell in them! But woe to you, O earth and sea, for the devil has come down to you in great wrath, because he knows that his time is short! (Rev 12:10-12)

This shows that it is only after Satan and his angels have been pushed out of the second heaven that the power, kingdom, and authority of Christ are fully restored in the second heaven. Having lost his position in the spiritual realms, the power of Satan to go before God to accuse was greatly whittled down. Recall that Satan was still going before God, when the sons of God gathered before him (as seen in Job). However, after his defeat in the second heaven, he is pushed down to the earth, where the next phase of the battle is to take place (we will see this in the coming chapters).

The second pointer to this is contained in the following verse: "For the accuser of our brothers has been thrown down, who accuses them day and night before our God. And *they have conquered him by the blood of the Lamb and by the word of their testimony, for they loved not their lives even unto death*" (Rev 12:11). The brethren conquer Satan through the blood of the Lamb and their testimony, even unto death. Clearly, this war in heaven referred to here is not a flashback of the previous war in heaven, because it is happening after the death of Christ (after the blood of the Lamb has been shed). Also, the people use their own testimonies and death (during the precursor period, when they will be persecuted) to conquer Satan. So, this is surely referring to the present generation of humans (the descendants of Adam—the Adamic race), who had not been created when the first war in heaven happened.

However, putting this back in context, following our logic and sequence of events, this particular war happens after the sixth seal is opened. This is way past the point where martyrs were seen in heaven crying to God for revenge:

> When he opened the fifth seal, I saw under the altar the souls of those who had been slain for the word of God and for the witness they had borne. (Rev 6:10)

Interestingly, those martyrs were slain because of their testimonies! And they were told to wait for more of their brethren to be slain for the same reason:

> Then they were each given a white robe and told to rest a little longer, *until the number of their fellow servants and their brothers should be complete, who were to be killed as they themselves had been*. (Rev 6:11)

Furthermore, before the dragon and his angels are thrown down to earth, the chief end-time character operating in the world and persecuting Christians and others who oppose his rule is the antichrist, a human possessed by Satan. Thus, Satan is in the spiritual realm, but his spirit is in the antichrist (more like trying to replicate the past scenario where the spirit of God was in Jesus Christ, while he was on earth). This way Satan still has his full spiritual capabilities while still influencing events on earth. However, when he is thrown down to earth, he becomes physically present on earth, hence can be dealt with like a man. This is the reason he will be conquered and bundled up like a man in the third angelic battle that will occur on earth (see §6.6.2).

4.4. UNDERSTANDING THE MYSTERY OF THE WOMAN AND THE DRAGON

> And a great sign appeared in heaven: a woman clothed with the sun, with the moon under her feet, and on her head a crown of twelve stars. [2] She was pregnant and was crying out in birth pains and the agony of giving birth. [3] And another sign appeared in heaven: behold, a great red dragon, with seven heads and ten horns, and on his heads seven diadems. [4] His tail swept down a third of the stars of heaven and cast them to the earth. And the dragon stood before the woman who was about to give birth, so that when she bore her child he might devour it. [5] She gave birth to a male child, one who is to rule all the nations with a rod of iron, but her child was caught up to God and to his throne, [6] and the woman fled into the wilderness, where she has a place prepared by God, in which she is to be nourished for 1,260 days. (Rev 12:1–6)

Revelation 12 presents a highly symbolized account of a fierce struggle between a woman and a dragon. To grasp the meaning of this passage, the true identities of the main characters represented symbolically need to be understood. To buttress that these are symbolic representations, the passage starts with "And *a great sign* appeared in heaven: a woman clothed with the sun, with *the moon under her feet*, and on her head a *crown of twelve stars*." Hence, it is a sign/symbol. Clearly, this is not a real woman or the Virgin Mary as most people tend to interpret it. The second verse further demonstrates this: "She was pregnant and was crying out in birth pains and the agony of giving birth." The woman here is the Christian church, and she is pregnant with Christians about to be delivered for Christ! Despite the fact that this symbolic event is situated right deep in the vision of Revelation John was given, many readers and Bible scholars tend to link this event to the birth of Jesus Christ. In actual sense, this verse is pointing to the end-time events, especially the period when the church will be going through the initial persecutions (birth-pain period—the actions of the four horsemen and the antichrist).

This is made evident as the sign of the dragon who had caused one third of the stars (angels) to be cast down to the earth:

> And another sign appeared in heaven: behold, a great red dragon, with seven heads and ten horns, and on his heads seven diadems. ⁴ His tail swept down a third of the stars of heaven and cast them to the earth. And the dragon stood before the woman who was about to give birth, so that when she bore her child he might devour it. (Rev 12:3–4)

This directly links to the point where Satan and his angels are chased down from the second heaven to the earth (§4.3), and he is so furious and is going after the church and her yet-to-be-born son:

> And when the dragon saw that he had been thrown down to the earth, he pursued the woman who had given birth to the male child. (Rev 12:13)

However, as soon as the woman goes through the birth pains and gives birth, her son is caught up to the throne of God:

> She gave birth to a male child, one who is to rule all the nations with a rod of iron, but her child was caught up to God and to his throne, ⁶ and the woman fled into the wilderness, where she has a place prepared by God, in which she is to be nourished for 1,260 days. (Rev 12:5–6)

This is clearly pointing to the great multitude (of souls) from all nations and languages found in heaven at the opening of the sixth seal, instead of the birth of Christ and escape of the holy family to Egypt. The woman/Christian church pregnant with Christians is undergoing persecution (birth pains) to purify them for God ("their clothes clean"). Satan wants to devour the souls of the Christian to deprive God. The goal of Satan and the antichrist in the end-time is to drag as many people as possible into their rebellious camp, whereas God's plan is to save as many souls as possible for the new kingdom he will establish on earth. Hence, the male child represents the souls of Christians and not Jesus Christ. One of the confusions that usually crops up here is the description of the male child as "one who is to rule all the nations with a rod of iron" (Rev 12:5). This is because this description is also attributed to Jesus Christ:

> From his mouth comes a sharp sword with which to strike down the nations, and he will rule them with a rod of iron. He will tread the winepress of the fury of the wrath of God the Almighty. (Rev 19:15)

However, the church in Thyatira is told that any of them who conquer the persecution of the antichrist without compromising their faith, will rule nations with a rod of iron:

> But to the rest of you in Thyatira, who do not hold this teaching, who have not learned what some call the deep things of Satan, to you I say, I do not lay on you any other burden. [25] Only hold fast what you have until I come. [26] The one who conquers and who keeps my works until the end, *to him I will give authority over the nations,* [27] *and he will rule them with a rod of iron,* as when earthen pots are broken in pieces, even as I myself have received authority from my Father. [28] And I will give him the morning star. [29] He who has an ear, let him hear what the Spirit says to the churches. (Rev 2:18–29)

This description closely matches the description of the male child delivered by the woman in Rev 12, rather than the description of Christ in Rev 19. The key difference is that Jesus Christ was given another attribute, in addition to ruling with an iron rod. He comes with a sword in his mouth, which he will use to slay nations:

> *From his mouth comes a sharp sword with which to strike down the nations,* and he will rule them with a rod of iron. (Rev 19:15)

Hence, soon after the stars fall from heaven, a great multitude of people who had gone through the persecutions were seen in the throne of God ("but her child was caught up to God and to his throne"). Compared to the birth of Christ, the events surrounding the birth of Christ showed that the entire family—the son, father, and mother—escaped to Egypt (which is really not a wilderness); but in the Rev 12 account, the son was separated from the mother—the son was caught up to God and his throne—and the mother was protected and nourished in the wilderness for another three and a half years (we shall see the reason for this in subsequent chapters—the church needed to be protected on the earth, as Christ was coming to establish his kingdom on earth). Furthermore, there is no mention of the father—Joseph—who was instrumental in the escape of the holy family to Egypt. Hence, the events described by John in Rev 12 are not a flashback to the events surrounding the birth of Christ and the persecution by Herod.

Putting all these together, it seems that Satan was patiently waiting in the second heaven to attack Christians; however, before he can strike, he is thrown down from his vantage point in the second heaven, alongside his angels, while the souls of Christians are taken to God. In fury he goes after the remnant of the church still on earth. However, the church is shielded from the wrath of Satan:

> And when the dragon saw that he had been thrown down to the earth, he pursued the woman who had given birth to the male child. ¹⁴ But the woman was given the two wings of the great eagle so that she might fly from the serpent into the wilderness, to the place where she is to be nourished for a time, and times, and half a time. ¹⁵ The serpent poured water like a river out of his mouth after the woman, to sweep her away with a flood. ¹⁶ But the earth came to the help of the woman, and the earth opened its mouth and swallowed the river that the dragon had poured from his mouth. (Rev 12:13–16)

In frustration he unleashes his anger on the Jews and the rest of Christians:

> Then the dragon became furious with the woman and went off to make war on the rest of her offspring, *on those who keep the commandments of God and hold to the testimony of Jesus*. And he stood on the sand of the sea. (Rev 12:17)

The clause "on those who keep the commandments of God and hold to the testimony of Jesus" points to the fact that the offspring being referred to here are the Jews who have been converted to Christianity (the commandment of God—law of Moses and testimony of Jesus). It is instructive to note that most Jews adhere only to the commandments of God; however, the two witnesses are sent to convert some Jews to the testimony of Christ—to believe that Jesus Christ is the Messiah that they have been waiting for. These Jews are the 144,000 that are sealed. They are sealed to protect them from the wrath of God that is to be unleashed on the inhabitants of the earth after many Christians have been killed or incarcerated. This description ("those who keep the commandments of God and hold to the testimony of Jesus") is used in other places in the book of Revelation. Chapter 5 will expound on this.

4.5. GOING INTO THE "WILDERNESS"

Just after Satan and his angels are cast down from the second heaven to the earth, there is a likelihood that an event will occur that will lead to some Christians being taken to a place of refuge somewhere on earth, where they will be protected from the wrath of Satan:

THE GREAT TRIBULATION

> And the dragon stood before the woman who was about to give birth, so that when she bore her child he might devour it. [5] She gave birth to a male child, one who is to rule all the nations with a rod of iron, but her child was caught up to God and to his throne, [6] and the *woman fled into the wilderness*, where she has a place prepared by God, in which she is to be nourished for 1,260 days. (Rev 12:4–6)

Even though placed at the twelfth chapter, far away from the sixth chapter where the sixth seal was opened, this event is part of the sixth seal event. Chronologically, it will happen immediately after Satan has been thrown down to earth alongside a third of angelic beings in the second heaven (see §4.3):

> And when the dragon saw that he had been thrown down to the earth, he pursued the woman who had given birth to the male child. [14] But the woman was given the two wings of the great eagle so that she might fly from the serpent into the wilderness, to the place where she is to be nourished for a time, and times, and half a time. [15] The serpent poured water like a river out of his mouth after the woman, to sweep her away with a flood. [16] But the earth came to the help of the woman, and the earth opened its mouth and swallowed the river that the dragon had poured from his mouth. [17] Then the dragon became furious with the woman and went off to make war on the rest of her offspring, on those who keep the commandments of God and hold to the testimony of Jesus. And he stood on the sand of the sea. (Rev 12:13–17)

Although the details are a bit sketchy, this passage suggests that the dragon will attempt to pursue the woman, but this will be thwarted/neutralized by God via supernatural means. It appears that the means of escape into the wilderness might be airplanes—"wings of the great eagle." Saint John may have described the aircraft as a great eagle because during the time the revelation was given to him (about two thousand years ago), there was no aircraft on earth, hence it would have been difficult for him to know exactly what he was being shown, to appropriately describe it. This escape might also be via other means facilitated supernaturally by angels. The reference to the "wings of the great eagle" might also be a spiritually symbolic use to represent God's facilitation of an escape to safety. In Exod 19, God stated that he facilitated the escape of Israelites from Egypt by bearing them on eagles' wings:

> Thus you shall say to the house of Jacob, and tell the children of Israel: ⁴ *"You have seen what I did to the Egyptians, and how I bore you on eagles' wings and brought you to Myself."* (Exod 19:3–4 NKJV)

There is little information on who will be able to make this trip, but the church in Philadelphia was promised an open door by Christ and that they would be kept from the hour of test coming upon the world:

> Behold, I have set before you an open door, which no one is able to shut. (Rev 3:8)

> Because you have kept my word about patient endurance, I will keep you from the hour of trial that is coming on the whole world, to try those who dwell on the earth. (Rev 3:10)

Hence, this suggests that Christians with attributes matching those of the church in Philadelphia may be taken to a place of refuge. The key difference between this and the conventional rapture theory is that going into the wilderness suggests a flight of Christians into some place of safety somewhere on earth beyond the reach of Satan, whereas rapture theory tend to suggest a literal translation of people (dead and living) from earth to heaven. Going by the conventional definition, rapture entails the translation of resurrected and transformed bodies into heaven, which is different from souls going into heaven, while the bodies remain on earth.

Jesus Christ also told his followers to flee to the wilderness/mountains once they see the abomination of desolation in Jerusalem:

> So when you see the abomination of desolation spoken of by the prophet Daniel, standing in the holy place (let the reader understand), ¹⁶ then let those who are in Judea flee to the mountains. ¹⁷ Let the one who is on the housetop not go down to take what is in his house, ¹⁸ and let the one who is in the field not turn back to take his cloak. (Matt 24:15–18)

He also in another place told disciples to flee from one town to the other:

> And you will be hated by all for my name's sake. But the one who endures to the end will be saved. ²³ When they persecute you in one town, flee to the next, for truly, I say to you, you will not have gone through all the towns of Israel before the Son of Man comes. (Matt 10:22–23)

If there is going to be a rapture, this would have been the right time for Christ to have mentioned it, rather than admonishing his followers to flee

THE GREAT TRIBULATION

into safety. He could not have painstakingly taken time to explain every key aspect of the end-time persecutions and tribulations, while leaving out an important aspect that would make the yoke lighter for his followers.

As a final word in this discussion, Jesus Christ was persecuted to death. He won his victory and crown by undergoing the pains of the cross. This was a standard he set up for his followers. Recall he had this to say:

> "If anyone would come after me, let him deny himself and take up his cross and follow me. [25] For whoever would save his life will lose it, but whoever loses his life for my sake will find it. [26] For what will it profit a man if he gains the whole world and forfeits his soul? Or what shall a man give in return for his soul? (Matt 16:24–26)

From the foregoing, it is amply clear that suffering and persecution have been established as a means of earning the heavenly crown promised to the followers of Christ. The apostles and disciples of Christ who are the forefathers of Christianity experienced severe persecutions, some of them losing their lives in brutal manner (martyrs of the church). This was the means they won their crowns of glory. Hence, if Jesus did not spare his apostles from such severe persecutions, which he established and also experienced, there is a slim chance he will spare Christians from the coming great tribulation through the rapture. He warned about this in John 15:

> Remember what I told you: "A servant is not greater than his master." *If they persecuted me, they will persecute you also.* (John 15:20 NIV)

To summarize, Jesus Christ expects his followers to accept the persecutions during the precursor period and use that as a means to testify for him across the world:

> [9] Then shall they deliver you up to be afflicted, and shall kill you: and ye shall be hated of all nations for my name's sake. [10] And then shall many be offended, and shall betray one another, and shall hate one another. [11] And many false prophets shall rise, and shall deceive many. [12] And because iniquity shall abound, the love of many shall wax cold. [13] But he that shall endure unto the end, the same shall be saved. [14] And this gospel of the kingdom shall be preached in all the world for a witness unto all nations; and then shall the end come. (Matt 24:9-14 AV)

However, he cautioned that Christians should run to safety once the abomination of desolation occurs:

> ¹⁵ When ye therefore shall see the abomination of desolation, spoken of by Daniel the prophet, stand in the holy place, (whoso readeth, let him understand:) ¹⁶ then let them which be in Judæa flee into the mountains: ¹⁷ let him which is on the housetop not come down to take anything out of his house: ¹⁸ neither let him which is in the field return back to take his clothes. (Matt 24:15-18 AV)

Christians are only expected to remain in hiding and not allow themselves to be drawn out or deceived by appearances of false Christ:

> 23 Then if any man shall say unto you, Lo, here is Christ, or there; believe it not. 24 For there shall arise false Christs, and false prophets, and shall shew great signs and wonders; insomuch that, if it were possible, they shall deceive the very elect. 25 Behold, I have told you before. 26 Wherefore if they shall say unto you, Behold, he is in the desert; go not forth: behold, he is in the secret chambers; believe it not. 27 For as the lightning cometh out of the east, and shineth even unto the west; so shall also the coming of the Son of man be. (Matt 24:23-27 AV)

They are to raise their heads again from their hiding place/s when they see Christ coming with his angels:

> 27 And then shall they see the Son of man coming in a cloud with power and great glory. 28 And when these things begin to come to pass, then look up, and lift up your heads; for your redemption draweth nigh. (Lk 21:27-28 AV)

4.6. THE EMPOWERMENT OF THE FIRST BEAST— THE REEMERGENCE OF THE ANTICHRIST

> And I saw a beast rising out of the sea, with ten horns and seven heads, with ten diadems on its horns and blasphemous names on its heads. ² And the beast that I saw was like a leopard; its feet were like a bear's, and its mouth was like a lion's mouth. And to it the dragon gave his power and his throne and great authority. ³ One of its heads seemed to have a mortal wound, but its mortal wound was healed, and the whole earth marveled as they followed the beast. ⁴ And they worshiped the dragon, for he had given his authority to the beast, and they worshiped the beast, saying, "Who is like the beast, and who can fight against it?"

> ⁵ And the beast was given a mouth uttering haughty and blasphemous words, and it was allowed to exercise authority for forty-two months. ⁶ It opened its mouth to utter blasphemies against God, blaspheming his name and his dwelling, that is, those who dwell in heaven. ⁷ Also it was allowed to make war on the saints and to conquer them. And authority was given it over every tribe and people and language and nation, ⁸ and all who dwell on earth will worship it, everyone whose name has not been written before the foundation of the world in the book of life of the Lamb who was slain. ⁹ If anyone has an ear, let him hear:
>
> ¹⁰ If anyone is to be taken captive, to captivity he goes; if anyone is to be slain with the sword, with the sword must he be slain. Here is a call for the endurance and faith of the saints. (Rev 13:1–10).

This event of the rising of the first beast chronologically follows from the last events of Rev 12. In the last paragraph of Rev 12, after the failed attempt of Satan to make war against the woman and her son, Satan goes after her other offspring:

> Then the dragon became furious with the woman and went off to make war on the rest of her offspring, on those who keep the commandments of God and hold to the testimony of Jesus. *And he stood on the sand of the sea.* (Rev 12:17)

We already understand from §4.2 that this other offspring of the woman is mainly the Jews. Precisely from Rev 12:17, the dragon/Satan goes to wait for the beast to rise from the sea. Thus, when the beast rises from the sea, Satan is already there waiting:

> And I saw a beast rising out of the sea, with ten horns and seven heads, with ten diadems on its horns and blasphemous names on its heads. ² And the beast that I saw was like a leopard; its feet were like a bear's, and its mouth was like a lion's mouth. And to it the dragon gave his power and his throne and great authority. (Rev 13:1–2)

This situates the time of this event narrated in Rev 13 to be soon after the fall of Satan and his angels to the earth from the second heaven and before the opening of the seventh seal.

The beast rising out of the sea does not necessarily suggest that a beast will appear from the coast. It most likely means that the beast will come from the earth. It is an earthbound entity. We gather this from Dan 7, when the same phrase was used for the four beasts, and interpretation was given to this effect by one of the heavenly beings that Daniel inquired from:

> ³ And four great beasts *came up out of the sea*, different from one another. (Dan 7:3)

> As for me, Daniel, my spirit within me was anxious, and the visions of my head alarmed me. ¹⁶ I approached one of those who stood there and asked him the truth concerning all this. So he told me and made known to me the interpretation of the things. ¹⁷ '*These four great beasts are four kings who shall arise out of the earth*.' (Dan 7:15–17)

This first beast appears to be both a system (antichrist system/government) as well as a character (the antichrist who will be leading this system). However, we already know that the antichrist emerged earlier on the world stage as the rider of the white horse (the opening of the first seal, which marked the beginning of the end-time events—see §2.2.1). So how come the antichrist/first beast is just rising from the sea at this point? The answer to this puzzle lies in the following verse:

> One of its heads seemed to have a mortal wound, but its mortal wound was healed, and the whole earth marveled as they followed the beast. (Rev 13:3)

This tends to suggest that the antichrist somehow may have been killed/severely wounded when the end-time geopolitical wars were raging (see §3.5.2) or his powers tremendously diminished, only for him to rise again, this time in his true nature of a beast, with more heads. Hence, this rising of the beast could actually be the empowerment of the antichrist by the red dragon. Revelation 13:14, while describing the second beast, disclosed the means the beast was wounded:

> It performs great signs, even making fire come down from heaven to earth in front of people, ¹⁴ and by the signs that it is allowed to work in the presence of the beast it deceives those who dwell on earth, telling them *to make an image for the beast that was wounded by the sword and yet lived*. (Rev 13:13–14)

This first beast matches the little horn that grew out of the fourth beast that Daniel saw:

> The first was like a lion and had eagles' wings. Then as I looked its wings were plucked off, and it was lifted up from the ground and made to stand on two feet like a man, and the mind of a

man was given to it. ⁵ And behold, another beast, a second one, like a bear. It was raised up on one side. It had three ribs in its mouth between its teeth; and it was told, "Arise, devour much flesh." ⁶ After this I looked, and behold, another, like a leopard, with four wings of a bird on its back. And the beast had four heads, and dominion was given to it. ⁷ After this I saw in the night visions, and behold, a fourth beast, terrifying and dreadful and exceedingly strong. It had great iron teeth; it devoured and broke in pieces and stamped what was left with its feet. It was different from all the beasts that were before it, and it had ten horns. ⁸ I considered the horns, and behold, there came up among them another horn, *a little one, before which three of the first horns were plucked up by the roots. And behold, in this horn were eyes like the eyes of a man, and a mouth speaking great things.* (Dan 7:4–9).

This second version of antichrist (empowered by Satan) is no longer pretending as it did in the previous stages but is poised to enforce the rule and authority of Satan, with gloves off and by any means possible.

A key point to note here is that the first beast is given forty-two months to exercise its authority:

> And the beast was given a mouth uttering haughty and blasphemous words, and it was allowed to exercise authority for forty-two months. (Rev 13:5)

This coincides with the same number of months the woman will be sheltered in the wilderness:

> And the woman fled into the wilderness, where she has a place prepared by God, in which she is to be nourished for 1,260 days [forty-two months]. (Rev 12:6)

Thus, this confirms that this event is occurring either alongside the wilderness event or immediately after it (see §4.3), and a long time before the opening of the seventh seal. Hence, as the woman is nourished in the wilderness, the antichrist exercises its wickedness across the world.

4.7. RISING OF THE SECOND BEAST— THE FALSE PROPHET

Then I saw another beast rising out of the earth. It had two horns like a lamb and it spoke like a dragon. ¹² It exercises all the

> authority of the first beast in its presence, and makes the earth and its inhabitants worship the first beast, whose mortal wound was healed. [13] It performs great signs, even making fire come down from heaven to earth in front of people, [14] and by the signs that it is allowed to work in the presence of the beast it deceives those who dwell on earth, telling them to make an image for the beast that was wounded by the sword and yet lived. [15] And it was allowed to give breath to the image of the beast, so that the image of the beast might even speak and might cause those who would not worship the image of the beast to be slain. [16] Also it causes all, both small and great, both rich and poor, both free and slave, to be marked on the right hand or the forehead, [17] so that no one can buy or sell unless he has the mark, that is, the name of the beast or the number of its name. [18] This calls for wisdom: let the one who has understanding calculate the number of the beast, for it is the number of a man, and his number is 666. (Rev 13:11–18)

The second beast introduced here is presented as the enforcer of the rule of the antichrist. It will be given power and authority to implement the dictates of the antichrist. In addition, it will devise various means, including signs and wonders, that it will use to deceive and make the people on earth at this time to worship the antichrist. Despite popular speculations, he may not necessarily be a religious leader. Many Bible scholars and preachers seem to think that the individual must be a religious leader to be able to make the people to worship the antichrist. But this does not necessarily hold true. considering what the verse says:

> It exercises all the authority of the first beast in its presence, and makes the earth and its inhabitants worship the first beast, whose mortal wound was healed. (Rev 13:12)

It is through the authority of the beast that he makes the earth and inhabitants to worship the beast. This suggests a compulsive/forceful worship of the beast, using the oppressive authority of the antichrist and not due to a religious authority the individual already has. Hence, this individual could be anybody, e.g., a tech giant, political leader, religious leader, diplomat, etc. As a matter of fact, technology may play a huge role in the implementation of the antichrist's policies. To confirm this, the passage notes that an image of the beast will be animated to the extent that it can speak and able to identify ("might cause") those who refuse to worship the beast, so they might be killed:

> And it was allowed to give breath to the image of the beast, so that the image of the beast might even speak and *might cause* those who would not worship the image of the beast to be slain. [16] Also it causes all, both small and great, both rich and poor, both free and slave, to be marked on the right hand or the forehead, [17] so that no one can buy or sell unless he has the mark, that is, the name of the beast or the number of its name. (Rev 13:12)

Hence, this individual also known as the false prophet could be one of the technology giants who can use technology to do a lot of wonders (calling down fire from heaven and making the image of the beast to speak, which could be accomplished with artificial intelligence, holograms, or other similar technology) and implement a digital identity technology that could be used to track and control human activities across the globe. This false prophet could also be a political or religious leader, with access to the relevant technologies. This could also be something mundane to the modern generation compared to how the generation of St. John might have viewed it. Many things currently considered mundane by this generation would have been considered mysteries by the past generations of humans.

One of the key highlights of this passage is the implementation of the mark of the beast. This has always terrified Christians, who are always watching out for anything that could be this mark. Across church history, various things have been suggested to be the mark, which ended up not to be. However, as we approach the end-time, this will become clearer. The book of Revelation seems to suggest that the sole purpose of the mark of the beast is to conclusively seal those who have pledged allegiance to Satan and the antichrist from receiving salvation, and to prevent those who have not pledged this allegiance to the antichrist from participating in economic activities (buying and selling) of the world controlled by the antichrist:

> Also it causes all, both small and great, both rich and poor, both free and slave to be *marked on the right hand or the forehead*, [17] so that no one can buy or sell unless he has the mark. (Rev 13:16–17)

A very significant point to note here is that the false prophet will emerge (start actions) on the world stage soon after the first beast (antichrist) has been revealed. This goes to counter various suggestions that certain individuals, especially religious leaders, are the false prophet. Although, currently, there are various candidates out there that could fit this description of the would-be false prophet, with views that are diametrically opposed to God and the teachings of Christ, that could lead people astray, it is only when the antichrist has been revealed to the world that the false prophet will be revealed. Hence, if this individual is currently present, he has not yet been empowered to act as the false prophet.

4.8. THE REVELATION OF MAN OF LAWLESSNESS

> Let no one deceive you in any way. For that day will not come, unless the rebellion comes first, and the man of lawlessness is revealed, the son of destruction, [4] who opposes and exalts himself against every so-called god or object of worship, so that he takes his seat in the temple of God, proclaiming himself to be God. (2 Thess 2:3–4)

In one of his letters to the church in Thessalonica, St. Paul mentioned the revelation of the man of lawlessness. This has become a key marker for determining when the antichrist (the man of lawlessness/son of perdition) will fully emerge from his shadows to show his true color to the world. Verse 4 is really instructive, as it clearly identifies the man of lawlessness as the antichrist and presents key attributes that will be used to determine who this man of lawlessness is, i.e., his revelation to the entire world:

> who opposes and exalts himself against every so-called god or object of worship, so that he takes his seat in the temple of God, proclaiming himself to be God. (2 Thess 2:4)

This individual will denounce and oppose any other god, in order to exalt himself as the God. This description matches the description of the actions of the first beast in Rev 13:

> It opened its mouth to utter blasphemies against God, blaspheming his name and his dwelling, that is, those who dwell in heaven. (Rev 13:6)

This event is particularly important because it will mark the beginning of the great tribulation with attacks primarily focused on Jews and Christians, who will oppose this individual, having realized who he is. The event that will reveal this individual as the antichrist will be his invasion of Jerusalem and his going into the temple of God to declare himself as God, while profaning the name of God and Jesus Christ. Christ told his followers to watch out for this event:

> So when you see the abomination of desolation spoken of by the prophet Daniel, standing in the holy place (let the reader understand). (Matt 24:15)

This reference by Christ to the abomination of desolation that Daniel spoke of is contained in Dan 9:

> Desolations are decreed. [27] And he shall make a strong covenant with many for one week, and for half of the week he shall put an end to sacrifice and offering. And on the wing of abominations shall come one who makes desolate, until the decreed end is poured out on the desolator. (Dan 9:26–27)

As well as Dan 11:

> For ships of Kittim shall come against him, and he shall be afraid and withdraw, and shall turn back and be enraged and take action against the holy covenant. He shall turn back and pay attention to those who forsake the holy covenant. [31] Forces from him shall appear and profane the temple and fortress, and shall take away the regular burnt offering. And they shall set up the abomination that makes desolate. (Dan 11:30–31)

While the various wars are raging around Israel (§3.5.2) and possibly across other parts of the world, the antichrist, despite his hatred for the Jews, will ignore Israel for a while, as he has made a covenant/deal with them (see §3.8). However, when he loses his last war with the "king of the South" (this may be a reference to Egypt) and withdraws, his rage against the Jews (who made a holy covenant with God through Abraham) will boil, and he will invade Jerusalem. This invasion of Jerusalem is captured in Revelation, as well as in the Gospels:

> Rise and measure the temple of God and the altar and those who worship there, [2] but do not measure the court outside the temple; leave that out, for it is given over to the nations, and they will trample the holy city for forty-two months. [3] And I will grant authority to my two witnesses, and they will prophesy for 1,260 days, clothed in sackcloth. (Rev 11:1–3)

> But when you see Jerusalem surrounded by armies, then know that its desolation has come near. [21] Then let those who are in Judea flee to the mountains, and let those who are inside the city depart, and let not those who are out in the country enter it, [22] for these are days of vengeance, to fulfill all that is written. [23] Alas for women who are pregnant and for those who are

> nursing infants in those days! For there will be great distress upon the earth and wrath against this people. [24] They will fall by the edge of the sword and be led captive among all nations, and Jerusalem will be trampled underfoot by the Gentiles, until the times of the Gentiles are fulfilled. (Luke 21:20–24)

This last battle between this individual and the king of the South that he lost might be the point he was mortally wounded but was revived by Satan who had just fallen from the second heaven (§§4.2 and 4.5). Hence, at this point, this individual who has been waging wars and amassing a lot of power will be revealed as the long-awaited antichrist to the entire world. Then will the great tribulation begin, accompanied by unprecedented deception and persecution:

> Then if anyone says to you, "Look, here is the Christ!" or "There he is!" do not believe it. [24] For false christs and false prophets will arise and perform great signs and wonders, so as to lead astray, if possible, even the elect. [25] See, I have told you beforehand. [26] So, if they say to you, "Look, he is in the wilderness," do not go out. If they say, "Look, he is in the inner rooms," do not believe it. [27] For as the lightning comes from the east and shines as far as the west, so will be the coming of the Son of Man. (Matt 24:15–27)

> The coming of the lawless one is by the activity of Satan with all power and false signs and wonders, [10] and with all wicked deception for those who are perishing, because they refused to love the truth and so be saved. [11] Therefore God sends them a strong delusion, so that they may believe what is false, [12] in order that all may be condemned who did not believe the truth but had pleasure in unrighteousness. (2 Thess 2:9–12)

The period the first beast is given to exercise its authority on earth also corresponds to the period that the desolator recorded in Daniel was allocated to act (42 months = 3.5 years; 1290 days = 42.4 months):

> And from the time that the regular burnt offering is taken away and the abomination that makes desolate is set up, there shall be 1,290 days. [12] Blessed is he who waits and arrives at the 1,335 days. (Dan 12:11–12)

Anyone on earth at this point should not contemplate on finding Jesus Christ anywhere on the earth, including the wilderness, at this time. The antichrist will devise many means at this time to simulate the second coming of Christ, knowing that once Christians realizes that the antichrist is on the world stage, they will expectantly be looking forward to the return of Jesus Christ. The antichrist will exploit this emotion to deceive many. Christ made it clear that his return will not be a hidden event, as all will see him come. Moreover, because the antichrist will be given about forty-two months (three and a half years to exercise his authority), no Christian should believe that Christ will immediately return once the antichrist's identity is revealed.

4.9. MAKING WAR AGAINST THE SAINTS

And the beast was given a mouth uttering haughty and blasphemous words, and it was *allowed to exercise authority for forty-two months.* ⁶ It opened its mouth to utter blasphemies against God, blaspheming his name and his dwelling, that is, those who dwell in heaven.
⁷ *Also it was allowed to make war on the saints and to conquer them.* And authority was given it over every tribe and people and language and nation, ⁸ and all who dwell on earth will worship it, everyone whose name has not been written before the foundation of the world in the book of life of the Lamb who was slain. ⁹ If anyone has an ear, let him hear:
¹⁰ If anyone is to be taken captive, to captivity he goes; if anyone is to be slain with the sword, with the sword must he be slain. Here is a call for the endurance and faith of the saints.
(Rev 13:1–10)

Following the revelation of the man of lawlessness will be the war against the saints. Once the antichrist and his army invade Jerusalem, he will launch a serious crackdown on the Jews and Christians. From this time onwards, he will have just forty-two months to operate and exercise his authority to the fullest over all nations until Jesus Christ returns to conquer him and his army.

4.10. THE GREAT TRIBULATION (THE WRATH OF THE DEVIL)

The great tribulation is the unprecedented persecution of Jews and followers of Christ by the agents of Satan, specifically, the antichrist and his horde of human and demonic armies. This period starts soon after the dragon is thrown down from the second heaven to the earth, and he is furious against those who obey the commandment of God and believe in the testimonies of Jesus Christ. This period corresponds with the time of Jacob's trouble, when Satan and antichrist turn against the Jews and Jerusalem. Recall that the persecution of believers, which intensifies during the fifth seal, is to continue in the sixth seal. At the end of the fifth seal, the martyrs already in heaven are told to be patient until more believers are killed:

> Then they were each given a white robe and told to rest a little longer, until the number of their fellow servants and their brothers should be complete, who were to be killed as they themselves had been. (Rev 6:11)

Hence, if more Christians are to be killed, that could only be happening during the sixth seal, after the dragon and his angels have been cast down on earth. This is the reason the voice in heaven declares:

> But woe to you, O earth and sea, for the devil has come down to you in great wrath, because he knows that his time is short! (Rev 12:12)

Hence, the subsequent appearance of the multitudes from every nation and tribe should not be surprising. But this also points to the intensity of the wrath of the dragon against believers, as multitudes will be killed in a very short time!

Thus, by the time many believers have been killed and the rest probably gone underground (the church goes underground—into the "wilderness"), the antichrist will focus more on the Jews!

> For there will be great distress upon the earth and wrath against this people. ^{24} They will fall by the edge of the sword and be led captive among all nations, and Jerusalem will be trampled underfoot by the Gentiles, until the times of the Gentiles are fulfilled. (Luke 21:23–24)

Also see:

> Behold, the day of the LORD cometh, and thy spoil shall be divided in the midst of thee. ^{2} For I will gather all nations against Jerusalem to battle; and the city shall be taken, and the houses rifled, and the women ravished; and half of the city shall go forth into captivity, and the residue of the people shall not be cut off from the city. ^{3} Then shall the LORD go forth, and fight against those nations, as when he fought in the day of battle. (Zech 14:1–3 AV)

4.11. WILL THERE BE CHRISTIANS ON EARTH WHEN THE DRAGON SHOWS UP?

There will be many Christians on the earth when the dragon shows up on the earth. However, there are some indications that some Christians will flee to a place of protection on the earth (see §4.3):

> And the woman fled into the wilderness, where she has a place prepared by God, in which she is to be nourished for 1,260 days. (Rev 12:6)

Other Christians who who may not make it to the wilderness will face the dragon and the antichrist during the great tribulation. This set of Christians can be saved only by their testimonies. Hence, any Christian who finds himself still on earth and within the reach of the antichrist should prepare to spread the gospel of Christ and face the consequences—imprisonment and/or death:

> If anyone is to be taken captive, to captivity he goes; if anyone is to be slain with the sword, with the sword must he be slain. Here is a call for the endurance and faith of the saints. (Rev 13:10)

Any believer who seeks to preserve his/her life at this period by shying away from preaching the gospel and Jesus Christ to the world will lose his/her eternal life:

> Whoever seeks to preserve his life will lose it, but whoever loses his life will keep it (Luke 17:33).

> These are the ones coming out of the great tribulation. They have washed their robes and made them white in the blood of the Lamb. (Rev 7:14)

> But watch yourselves lest your hearts be weighed down with dissipation and drunkenness and cares of this life, and that day come upon you suddenly like a trap. [35] For it will come upon all who dwell on the face of the whole earth. [36] But stay awake at all times, praying that you may have strength to escape all these things that are going to take place, and to stand before the Son of Man. (Luke 21:34–36)

As a matter of fact, God expects believers to give up their lives:

> And I heard a voice from heaven saying, "Write this: Blessed are the dead who die in the Lord from now on." "Blessed indeed,"

says the Spirit, "that they may rest from their labors, for their deeds follow them!" (Rev 14:13)

4.12. A GREAT MULTITUDE FROM EVERY NATION

After this I looked, and behold, a great multitude that no one could number, from every nation, from all tribes and peoples and languages, standing before the throne and before the Lamb, clothed in white robes, with palm branches in their hands, [10] and crying out with a loud voice, "Salvation belongs to our God who sits on the throne, and to the Lamb!" [11] And all the angels were standing around the throne and around the elders and the four living creatures, and they fell on their faces before the throne and worshiped God, [12] saying, "Amen! Blessing and glory and wisdom and thanksgiving and honor and power and might be to our God forever and ever! Amen."

[13] Then one of the elders addressed me, saying, "Who are these, clothed in white robes, and from where have they come?" [14] I said to him, "Sir, you know." And he said to me, "These are the ones coming out of the great tribulation. They have washed their robes and made them white in the blood of the Lamb.

[15] "Therefore they are before the throne of God, and serve him day and night in his temple; and he who sits on the throne will shelter them with his presence.

[16] They shall hunger no more, neither thirst anymore; the sun shall not strike them, nor any scorching heat.

[17] For the Lamb in the midst of the throne will be their shepherd, and he will guide them to springs of living water, and God will wipe away every tear from their eyes." (Rev 7:9–17)

There seems to be a sudden appearance of a great multitude from every part of the earth in heaven. The Bible does not provide any detail on the process that brings such a multitude to heaven. This has essentially been a subject of several conjectures and at times a source of confusion. It seems that God purposely left out the details for Christians to figure it out from various pointers in the Bible. The main confusion in understanding this stems from the fact that many Bible translations use the phrase "coming out of the great tribulation" (Rev 7:14); however some translations, such as the New Living Translation, translate this phrase ("coming out") as "died":

> Then he said to me, "These are the ones who died in the great tribulation. They have washed their robes in the blood of the Lamb and made them white." (Rev 7:14 NLT)

There are other Bible translations that do not use "come" or "coming out." For instance, the Contemporary English Version translates the verse as:

> These are the ones who have gone through the great suffering. They have washed their robes in the blood of the Lamb and have made them white. (Rev 7:14 CEV)

The Weymouth New Testament translates this as:

> "They are those," he said, "who have just passed through the great distress, and have washed their robes and made them white in the blood of the Lamb." (Rev 7:14 Weymouth NT)

The great tribulation happened on the earth, and the standard way for people to go from earth to heaven is via death. This implies that the great multitude seen in heaven must be the souls of the people who have died on earth. Hence, this great multitude of people seen in heaven are martyred. Recall that at the opening of the fifth seal, some martyrs were seen in heaven, and they pleaded for revenge against those who killed them on earth. And they were told to be patient for more of their brethren to be killed before the world is judged and their death avenged:

> Then they were each given a white robe and told to rest a little longer, *until the number of their fellow servants and their brothers should be complete, who were to be killed as they themselves had been.* (Rev 6:11).

Hence, the great multitude seen afterwards in heaven are the ones that will make up the number of people that are to be killed. Furthermore, the wrath of God on the earth started in the seventh seal, soon after the great multitude were seen in heaven, thus aligning perfectly with the promise that was made in the fifth seal that the earth will be judged once the number of martyrs to be killed has been completed. It is also remarkable that the souls that were seen in the fifth seal were given white robes to wear while they waited, and the great multitude seen in heaven are also donning white robes. This couldn't be any clearer!

Another salient point to note is the fact that the great multitude comes "from every nation, from all tribes and peoples and languages." This suggests that the reach of the antichrist is global and not just around the Middle East.

5

The Seventh Seal: The Wrath of God

5.1. ANNOUNCING THE COMING WRATH OF GOD AND JESUS CHRIST—"THE GREAT DAY OF THEIR WRATH HAS COME"

> The sky vanished like a scroll that is being rolled up, and every mountain and island was removed from its place. [15] Then the kings of the earth and the great ones and the generals and the rich and the powerful, and everyone, slave and free, hid themselves in the caves and among the rocks of the mountains, [16] calling to the mountains and rocks, "Fall on us and hide us from the face of him who is seated on the throne, and from the wrath of the Lamb, [17] for the great day of their wrath has come, and who can stand?" (Rev 6:14–17)

The opening of the sixth seal reveals what seems to be an upheaval in the heavens, with the stars of the sky falling to earth. This scene captures the point Satan and his army are defeated and chased out of their heavenly abode after the fierce war in the second heaven (see §4.3). It seems that God will briefly reveal himself to the world at this point:

> The sky vanished like a scroll that is being rolled up. (Rev 6:14)

The inhabitants of the earth see God seated on his throne, as they proclaim:

> hide us from the face of *him who is seated on the throne*, and from the wrath of the Lamb. (Rev 6:16)

The kings of the earth and the great ones (these are probably the spiritual beings—principalities, powers, thrones, etc.—who had rebelled against God at one time or the other) know that their time to face the music has come, hence their attempt to hide from God:

> Fall on us and hide us from the face of him who is seated on the throne, and from *the wrath of the Lamb*, [17] for the great day of their wrath has come, and who can stand? (Rev 6:16–17)

This reference to the "wrath of the Lamb" is pointing to the coming punishment Christ and his angels will unleash on Satan and his agents for their wicked acts on Christ's followers. Note that this wrath is actually the combination of the wrath of God (one seated on the throne) and that of Jesus Christ (the wrath of the Lamb)—"for the great day of *their* wrath has come, and who can stand?"

Despite the fact that this proclamation is made in the sixth seal, the actual event (the unleashing of God's wrath on Satan and his followers on earth) is to commence during the seventh seal, after Satan and the antichrist have been given free reign to exercise their full powers on the earth.

5.2. THE SEALING OF THE 144,000 JEWS

> After this I saw four angels standing at the four corners of the earth, holding back the four winds of the earth, that no wind might blow on earth or sea or against any tree. [2] Then I saw another angel ascending from the rising of the sun, with the seal of the living God, and he called with a loud voice to the four angels who had been given power to harm earth and sea, [3] saying, "Do not harm the earth or the sea or the trees, until we have sealed the servants of our God on their foreheads." [4] And I heard the number of the sealed, 144,000, sealed from every tribe of the sons of Israel:
>
> [5] 12,000 from the tribe of Judah were sealed, 12,000 from the tribe of Reuben, 12,000 from the tribe of Gad, [6] 12,000 from the tribe of Asher, 12,000 from the tribe of Naphtali, 12,000 from the tribe of Manasseh, [7] 12,000 from the tribe of Simeon, 12,000 from the tribe of Levi, 12,000 from the tribe of Issachar, [8] 12,000 from the tribe of Zebulun,12,000 from the tribe of Joseph, 12,000 from the tribe of Benjamin were sealed. (Rev 7:1–8)

THE SEVENTH SEAL: THE WRATH OF GOD

Towards the end of the events of the sixth seal and in preparation for the unleashing of the wrath of God, a seal is placed on a certain number of people from the Jewish stock. This is happening on the heels of the declaration by the rulers of the earth that the wrath of God upon earth is imminent (§5.1). As a matter of fact, the angels that will unleash this wrath on earth are already in place at this time:

> After this I saw four angels standing at the four corners of the earth, holding back the four winds of the earth, that no wind might blow on earth or sea or against any tree. (Rev 7:1)

> And he called with a loud voice to the four angels who had been given power to harm earth and sea, ³ saying, "Do not harm the earth or the sea or the trees, until we have sealed the servants of our God on their foreheads." (Rev 7:2–3)

This is a critical moment in the end-time events, when God will take a protective measure to safeguard a limited number (144,000) of people from Israel. At this point many Christians would have been killed, imprisoned, or gone underground amidst increasing persecution of the antichrist. The Jews are essentially being sealed so that they will not feel the impact as the wrath of God is reeled out. This is similar to what happened in Egypt on the Passover night (Exod 12:11–13), when the blood on the doorposts of Israelites prevented them from being killed by the angel of God as he passed through Egypt executing God's judgment.

It is instructive to note that the sealing of the 144,000 Jews and the appearance of the great multitude in heaven happen prior to the opening of the seventh seal (the period marking the wrath of God on earth).

5.3. JUDGMENT ON THE NATIONS

> Come near, ye nations, to hear; and hearken, ye people: let the earth hear, and all that is therein; the world, and all things that come forth of it. ² For the indignation of the Lord is upon all nations, and his fury upon all their armies: he hath utterly destroyed them, he hath delivered them to the slaughter. ³ Their slain also shall be cast out, and their stink shall come up out of their carcases, and the mountains shall be melted with their blood.⁴ And all the host of heaven shall be dissolved, and the heavens shall be rolled together as a scroll: and all their host shall fall down, as the leaf falleth off from the vine, and as a falling fig from the fig tree. ⁵ For my sword shall be bathed in

> heaven: behold, it shall come down upon Idumea, and upon the people of my curse, to judgment. ⁶ The sword of the Lord is filled with blood, it is made fat with fatness, and with the blood of lambs and goats, with the fat of the kidneys of rams: for the Lord hath a sacrifice in Bozrah, and a great slaughter in the land of Idumea. ⁷ And the unicorns shall come down with them, and the bullocks with the bulls; and their land shall be soaked with blood, and their dust made fat with fatness. ⁸ For it is the day of the Lord's vengeance, and the year of recompences for the controversy of Zion. (Isa 34:1–8 AV)

The wrath of God is essentially a judgment of nations who maltreated God's people over the years. God had patiently waited for Satan to unleash all his wickedness on God's people, so as to render an appropriate judgment against him and his followers. This judgment was long foretold by many prophets of old, including Isaiah:

> For the LORD is enraged against all the nations, and furious against all their host; he has devoted them to destruction, has given them over for slaughter. (Isa 34:2)

The prophecy presented in Isa 34 closely matches what John saw and relayed in Revelation (see §§4.1 and 4.2). Starting from events of the sixth seal, when the host of heaven (most likely referring to angelic beings loyal to Satan) were cast down to earth:

> All the host of heaven shall rot away, and the skies roll up like a scroll. All their host shall fall, as leaves fall from the vine, like leaves falling from the fig tree. ⁵ For my sword has drunk its fill in the heavens. (Isa 34:4–5)

5.4. THE SEVENTH SEAL—COMMENCEMENT OF THE WRATH OF GOD

When the Lamb opened the seventh seal, there was silence in heaven for about half an hour. ² Then I saw the seven angels who stand before God, and seven trumpets were given to them. ³ And another angel came and stood at the altar with a golden censer, and he was given much incense to offer with the prayers of all the saints on the golden altar before the throne, ⁴ and the smoke of the incense, with the prayers of the saints, rose before God from the hand of the angel. ⁵ Then the angel took the censer

THE SEVENTH SEAL: THE WRATH OF GOD 103

> and filled it with fire from the altar and threw it on the earth, and there were peals of thunder, rumblings,[j] flashes of lightning, and an earthquake. (Rev 8:1–5)

The events accompanying the opening of the seventh seal are remarkably different from the events of the previous seals. The seventh seal marks the end of the great tribulation and the beginning of another phase in the end-time event, the wrath of God period. The severity of this phase can be glimpsed from the eerie and solemn silence experienced in heaven when the seal was opened:

> When the Lamb opened the seventh seal, there was silence in heaven for about half an hour. (Rev 8:1–2)

This stage, although marking the last of the seals, opens another era of sub-events that can be categorized as the seven trumpets period:

> Then I saw the seven angels who stand before God, and seven trumpets were given to them. (Rev 8:2)

This marks the beginning of the nested sequence of events discussed in §1.6. With the blowing of each trumpet, a particular event or punishment will be unleashed on the earth and its inhabitants. The blowing of the trumpets commences after an eighth angel throws a golden censer filled with fire from the altar of God on the earth:

> And another angel came and stood at the altar with a golden censer, and he was given much incense to offer with the prayers of all the saints on the golden altar before the throne, [4] and the smoke of the incense, with the prayers of the saints, rose before God from the hand of the angel. [5] Then the angel took the censer and filled it with fire from the altar and threw it on the earth, and there were peals of thunder, rumblings, flashes of lightning, and an earthquake. (Rev 8:3–5)

The seven trumpets period could broadly be split into two stages: the wrath on the physical and astronomic environment of the earth (first to fourth trumpets) and the wrath on the people (fifth to seventh trumpets). Although the duration of the events of each of the trumpets is not clearly specified, other than that of the fifth trumpet (where the demons are allowed five months to torment humanity), it may seem that some of the events are prolonged while others are swiftly carried out.

5.5. THE FIRST TRUMPET—WRATH ON THE TERRESTRIAL ENVIRONMENT

> Now the seven angels who had the seven trumpets prepared to blow them. ⁷ The first angel blew his trumpet, and there followed hail and fire, mixed with blood, and these were thrown upon the earth. And a third of the earth was burned up, and a third of the trees were burned up, and all green grass was burned up. (Rev 8:6–7)

The punishment unleashed at the blowing of the first trumpet appears to be targeted at the terrestrial parts of the earth: land, forest, and grassland. One-third of each of these is burned by the hail of fire unleashed from heaven.

5.6. THE SECOND TRUMPET—WRATH ON THE OCEANIC ENVIRONMENT

> The second angel blew his trumpet, and something like a great mountain, burning with fire, was thrown into the sea, and a third of the sea became blood. ⁹ A third of the living creatures in the sea died, and a third of the ships were destroyed. (Rev 8:8–9)

The punishment at this stage seems to be targeted at the oceanic environment—sea, oceanic creatures, and vessels sailing in these environments (ships). The agent of punishment seems to be a gigantic asteroid ("something like a great mountain, burning with fire") that will hit this environment. As usual with this series of events, its impact affects one-third of the environment and creatures in it.

5.7. THE THIRD TRUMPET—WRATH AGAINST FRESHWATER

> The third angel blew his trumpet, and a great star fell from heaven, blazing like a torch, and it fell on a third of the rivers and on the springs of water. ¹¹ The name of the star is Wormwood. A third of the waters became wormwood, and many people died from the water, because it had been made bitter. (Rev 8:10–11)

This event is targeting the fresh waters around the globe, an important natural resource for humans. The great star used here might be an asteroid or a meteoroid that pollutes the environment (with high concentration of a chemical depicted here as wormwood—a bitter "native to temperate regions of Eurasia and North Africa").[1] This pollution of one-third of freshwater would be so devastating, disrupting global freshwater supply that it would lead to the death of many people.

5.8. THE FOURTH TRUMPET—WRATH ON ASTRONOMIC BODIES

> The fourth angel blew his trumpet, and a third of the sun was struck, and a third of the moon, and a third of the stars, so that a third of their light might be darkened, and a third of the day might be kept from shining, and likewise a third of the night. (Rev 8:12)

This event targets key astronomic bodies: sun, moon, and stars and affects one-third of each of them. At this stage, the earth will be plunged into partial darkness. The diminished intensity of light will potentially reduce food production on earth, which could result in severe food shortages.

5.9. THE "WOE! WOE!! WOE!!!" PERIOD

> Then I looked, and I heard an eagle crying with a loud voice as it flew directly overhead, "Woe, woe, woe to those who dwell on the earth, at the blasts of the other trumpets that the three angels are about to blow!" (Rev 8:13)

Revelation 8 ends with warning of a crying eagle announcing that grievous calamity was about to befall the people on earth. This eagle is possibly symbolic of an angelic being that looks like an eagle. Recall that one of the seraphim surrounding the throne of God is described as looking like an eagle (see §3.1.1):

> And around the throne, on each side of the throne, are four living creatures, full of eyes in front and behind: [7] the first living creature like a lion, the second living creature like an ox, the third living creature with the face of a man, *and the fourth living creature like an eagle in flight.* (Rev 4:6–7)

---

1. Ugfacts, "Where to Buy Wormwood."

This is a very serious moment. Compared to the first four trumpets, which unleash events that target the earth's physical and astronomic environments, this phase of the trumpets will unleash terror and punishment on the people. The reason an angelic being is sent out to make this public proclamation is to forewarn the people of impending doom.

5.10. THE FIFTH TRUMPET (FIRST WOE)—THE TORMENT OF UNSEALED PEOPLE

And the fifth angel blew his trumpet, and I saw a star fallen from heaven to earth, and he was given the key to the shaft of the bottomless pit.² He opened the shaft of the bottomless pit, and from the shaft rose smoke like the smoke of a great furnace, and the sun and the air were darkened with the smoke from the shaft. ³ Then from the smoke came locusts on the earth, and they were given power like the power of scorpions of the earth. ⁴ They were told not to harm the grass of the earth or any green plant or any tree, but only those people who do not have the seal of God on their foreheads. ⁵ They were allowed to torment them for five months, but not to kill them, and their torment was like the torment of a scorpion when it stings someone. ⁶ And in those days people will seek death and will not find it. They will long to die, but death will flee from them.

⁷ In appearance the locusts were like horses prepared for battle: on their heads were what looked like crowns of gold; their faces were like human faces, ⁸ their hair like women's hair, and their teeth like lions' teeth; ⁹ they had breastplates like breastplates of iron, and the noise of their wings was like the noise of many chariots with horses rushing into battle. ¹⁰ They have tails and stings like scorpions, and their power to hurt people for five months is in their tails. ¹¹ They have as king over them the angel of the bottomless pit. His name in Hebrew is Abaddon, and in Greek he is called Apollyon.

¹² The first woe has passed; behold, two woes are still to come. (Rev 9:1–11)

The events of the fifth trumpet start with a star given a key to open the bottomless pit (Tartarus, a holding place for wicked demonic beings and fallen angels):

I saw a star fallen from heaven to earth, and he was given the key to the shaft of the bottomless pit. (Rev 9:1)

The identity of this star is not disclosed; however, the verse leaves relevant clues that could be used to identify on which side this angel is. The term "a star fallen from heaven to earth" shows that this being must be one of the angels that was cast out of the second heaven to the earth during the second war in heaven (see §4.2). This is made clearer in other Bible translations:

> Then the fifth angel blew his trumpet, and *I saw one who had fallen to earth from heaven*, and to him was given the key to the bottomless pit. (LB)

> And the fifth messenger did sound, *and I saw a star out of the heaven having fallen to the earth*, and there was given to it the key of the pit of the abyss. (YLT)

> Then the fifth angel blew his trumpet, and *I saw a star that had fallen to earth from the sky*, and he was given the key to the shaft of the bottomless pit. (NLT)

Having meted out some measures of God's wrath on various aspects of the terrestrial and marine environments in the preceding trumpets, the purpose of the fifth trumpet is to target the people still on earth. To understand this chapter, it is important to recall that this is happening under the fifth trumpet, which is part of the events of the seventh seal. At this point, only a few Christians are still on earth and would have gone underground, hiding from the persecutions of the antichrist. The people remaining on earth at this time will include the 144,000 Jews who have been sealed by the angel (see §5.2). They were sealed to protect them from the destructive events and torments that were to come on the earth from the opening of the seventh seal. Thus, at this stage the locusts (possibly demons) from the bottomless pit are unleashed on earth to torment every human being on earth (except those sealed) for five months

> They were told not to harm the grass of the earth or any green plant or any tree, but only those people who do not have the seal of God on their foreheads. (Rev 9:4)

Abaddon/Apollyon, the principality in charge of the bottomless pit, is the king of these demons that torment people for five months. Hence, this will be the time that Apollyon will rise! This stage also marks the end of the first woe that the eagle cried out at the end of the events of the fourth trumpet (§5.9).

5.11. THE SIXTH TRUMPET—KILLING OF ONE THIRD OF MANKIND (THE SECOND WOE)

> Then the sixth angel blew his trumpet, and I heard a voice from the four horns of the golden altar before God, [14] saying to the sixth angel who had the trumpet, "Release the four angels who are bound at the great river Euphrates." [15] So the four angels, who had been prepared for the hour, the day, the month, and the year, were released to kill a third of mankind. [16] The number of mounted troops was twice ten thousand times ten thousand; I heard their number. [17] And this is how I saw the horses in my vision and those who rode them: they wore breastplates the color of fire and of sapphire and of sulfur, and the heads of the horses were like lions' heads, and fire and smoke and sulfur came out of their mouths. [18] By these three plagues a third of mankind was killed, by the fire and smoke and sulfur coming out of their mouths. [19] For the power of the horses is in their mouths and in their tails, for their tails are like serpents with heads, and by means of them they wound.
> The rest of mankind, who were not killed by these plagues, did not repent of the works of their hands nor give up worshiping demons and idols of gold and silver and bronze and stone and wood, which cannot see or hear or walk, [21] nor did they repent of their murders or their sorceries or their sexual immorality or their thefts. (Rev 9:13–21)

After the initial torments of the first woe that last for five months, the people on earth are subjected to a further round of punishment, more intense than the previous one, leading to the death of one-third of the world population at this time. The main characters of the events of this period are four angels that were bound at the great river Euphrates. It is instructive to note that these four angels are released by the angel who blows the sixth trumpet. It is not clear from the verse if these angels are of God or Satan. However, they are either bad or so destructive in nature that they have to be restrained (bound) until the appropriate time for their actions:

> So the four angels, who had been prepared for the hour, the day, the month, and the year, were released to kill a third of mankind. (Rev 9:15)

It may also be that they had previously fallen and have been undergoing imprisonment like Abaddon, and are only released to take their last action against humanity at a specific time. The angels accomplish the task of killing one-third of the remaining human population by unleashing two hundred million soldiers:

> The number of mounted troops was twice ten thousand times ten thousand; I heard their number. (Rev 9:16)

The description of the horses the soldiers mount seems more like a military tank that is spitting out fire, smoke, and sulphur. It must be considered that John while seeing this vision could have thought that the military tanks were horses. It may have been impossible for him to describe a future technology using the language/parlance at his time (the first century AD, when motorized vehicles, guns, missiles did not exist). This passage could also mean that the four angels will instigate war/s that involve two hundred million soldiers and results in the death of one-third of humanity. A key point to note here is that despite the destructive events of the first and second woes, the people still on earth refuse to repent of their sins:

> The rest of mankind, who were not killed by these plagues, did not repent of the works of their hands nor give up worshiping demons and idols of gold and silver and bronze and stone and wood, which cannot see or hear or walk, [21] nor did they repent of their murders or their sorceries or their sexual immorality or their thefts. (Rev 9:20–21)

This could be due to the fact that the earth at this period will be infested with many wicked demons that have been released from the bottomless pit, as well as the powers and principalities that fell with Satan from the second heaven (see §4.3). Hence, many people will be possessed by demons and others enticed by the principalities and powers. This will be a very terrible time, with demons and fallen angels running haywire on earth.

5.12. THE TWO WITNESSES

> Then I was given a measuring rod like a staff, and I was told, "Rise and measure the temple of God and the altar and those who worship there, [2] but do not measure the court outside the temple; leave that out, for it is given over to the nations, and they will trample the holy city for forty-two months. [3] And I will grant authority to my two witnesses, and they will prophesy for 1,260 days, clothed in sackcloth."
>
> [4]These are the two olive trees and the two lampstands that stand before the Lord of the earth. [5] And if anyone would harm them, fire pours from their mouth and consumes their foes.

> If anyone would harm them, this is how he is doomed to be killed. [6] They have the power to shut the sky, that no rain may fall during the days of their prophesying, and they have power over the waters to turn them into blood and to strike the earth with every kind of plague, as often as they desire. [7] And when they have finished their testimony, the beast that rises from the bottomless pit will make war on them and conquer them and kill them, [8] and their dead bodies will lie in the street of the great city that symbolically is called Sodom and Egypt, where their Lord was crucified. [9] For three and a half days some from the peoples and tribes and languages and nations will gaze at their dead bodies and refuse to let them be placed in a tomb, [10] and those who dwell on the earth will rejoice over them and make merry and exchange presents, because these two prophets had been a torment to those who dwell on the earth. [11] But after the three and a half days a breath of life from God entered them, and they stood up on their feet, and great fear fell on those who saw them. [12] Then they heard a loud voice from heaven saying to them, "Come up here!" And they went up to heaven in a cloud, and their enemies watched them. [13] And at that hour there was a great earthquake, and a tenth of the city fell. Seven thousand people were killed in the earthquake, and the rest were terrified and gave glory to the God of heaven.
>
> [14] The second woe has passed; behold, the third woe is soon to come. (Rev 11:1–14)

In this passage two individuals referred to as two witnesses are introduced. These two witnesses are prophets who will be proselytizing/witnessing for God in Jerusalem. There are various speculations on the identity of these two individuals. Some believe they might be Moses and Elijah; others think they might be Elijah and John the Baptist or some other ancient prophets. But whoever they are, these prophets will be individuals that the Israelites can recognize and whose authority they can respect. They will be so powerful that they will be able to do a lot of wonderous things:

> Fire pours from their mouth and consumes their foes. If anyone would harm them, this is how he is doomed to be killed. [6] They have the power to shut the sky, that no rain may fall during the days of their prophesying, and they have power over the waters to turn them into blood and to strike the earth with every kind of plague, as often as they desire. (Rev 11:5–6)

Revelation 11 suggests that the two witnesses are killed within the sixth trumpet period. However, it is not explicitly stated when they begin to prophesy, other than the fact that they are given 1,260 days (41.4 months) to prophesy:

> Then I was given a measuring rod like a staff, and I was told, "Rise and measure the temple of God and the altar and those who worship there, ² but do not measure the court outside the temple; leave that out, for it is given over to the nations, and they will trample the holy city for forty-two months. ³ And I will grant authority to my two witnesses, and they will prophesy for 1,260 days, clothed in sackcloth." (Rev 11:1–3)

From the above passage, it could be seen that by the time John was given the measuring rod to demarcate the temple and altar from the rest of the temple area (outside courts), the antichrist and his army are yet to invade Jerusalem, and the two witnesses are not yet on the stage. This was added to help the reader to understand the activity of witnesses will either coincide with invasion of Jerusalem by the antichrist and his soldiers or closely follow it. The antichrist will trample on Jerusalem for 42 months, and the two witnesses will prophesy for 41.4 months (1,260 days):

> But do not measure the court outside the temple; leave that out, for it is given over to the nations, and they will trample the holy city for forty-two months. ³ And I will grant authority to my two witnesses, and they will prophesy for 1,260 days, clothed in sackcloth."(Rev 11:2–3)

Hence, it may be safe to assume that the two witnesses start prophesying soon after the abomination of desolation (§4.6), after the antichrist has been revealed and Jerusalem invaded by the antichrist and his army, and prophesy all through the period till the end of the sixth trumpet period, when they are eventually killed. In fact, the Bible indicates that their death and resurrection mark the end of the sixth trumpet, a.k.a. second woe:

> And at that hour there was a great earthquake, and a tenth of the city fell. Seven thousand people were killed in the earthquake, and the rest were terrified and gave glory to the God of heaven. ¹⁴ *The second woe has passed; behold, the third woe is soon to come.* (Rev 11:13–14)

The two witnesses are sent to preach to the Jews and bring them back to God by convincing them that Jesus Christ is the Messiah they have long waited for. In their doing so, the entire world is also being called to come to God and given the opportunity to repent. This period was also touched on by Daniel:

> Forces from him shall appear and profane the temple and fortress, and shall take away the regular burnt offering. And they shall set up the abomination that makes desolate. ³² He shall seduce with flattery those who violate the covenant, but the people who know their God shall stand firm and take action. ³³ *And the wise among the people shall make many understand, though for some days they shall stumble by sword and flame, by captivity and plunder.* ³⁴ When they stumble, they shall receive a little help. And many shall join themselves to them with flattery, ³⁵ and some of the wise shall stumble, so that they may be refined, purified, and made white, until the time of the end, for it still awaits the appointed time. (Dan 11:31–35)

Despite preaching only in Jerusalem, the activities of the two witnesses will probably be made visible to the rest of the world via modern communication technology (satellite television broadcast, internet, social media). This is because it is indicated that the people on earth are rejoicing over the death of the two witnesses who have been tormenting them:

> And those who dwell on the earth will rejoice over them and make merry and exchange presents, because these two prophets had been a torment to those who dwell on the earth. (Rev 11:10)

Another point to highlight here is the killer of the two witnesses. Revelation identifies him as "the beast that rises from the bottomless pit":

> And when they have finished their testimony, the beast that rises from the bottomless pit will make war on them and conquer them and kill them, and their dead bodies will lie in the street of the great city that symbolically is called Sodom and Egypt, where their Lord was crucified. (Rev 11:7–8)

It is difficult to say for sure if this is Abaddon, who is the fallen angel released from the bottomless pit (Rev 9:11), or the first beast of Rev 13 (the antichrist). The issue here is that that beast rises from the sea and not from the bottomless pit ("And I saw a beast rising out of the sea, with ten horns and seven heads, with ten diadems on its horns and blasphemous names on its heads"), whereas Abaddon is described as an angel and not a beast. It may be that the physical appearance of Abaddon is also like a beast. Saint John might be leaving a clue here that may be useful in understanding some of the events. This beast might also be the scarlet beast upon which the great prostitute rides (Rev 17). The beast is described as having risen from the bottomless pit. However, if this beast that kills the two witnesses is the antichrist, it means that the antichrist spirit comes from the bottomless pit.

5.13. THE REDEMPTION OF THE 144,000

> Then I looked, and behold, on Mount Zion stood the Lamb, and with him 144,000 who had his name and his Father's name written on their foreheads. ² And I heard a voice from heaven like the roar of many waters and like the sound of loud thunder. The voice I heard was like the sound of harpists playing on their harps, ³ and they were singing a new song before the throne and before the four living creatures and before the elders. No one could learn that song except the 144,000 who had been redeemed from the earth. ⁴ It is these who have not defiled themselves with women, for they are virgins. It is these who follow the Lamb wherever he goes. These have been redeemed from mankind as firstfruits for God and the Lamb, ⁵ and in their mouth no lie was found, for they are blameless. (Rev 14:1–5)

At the end of the events of the sixth trumpet and before the pouring of the last wrath of God on earth (the seven bowls), it seems that all the 144,000 Jews will have been killed (redeemed from the earth). This can be glimpsed from Rev 14 and 15. In Rev 14, the 144,000 Jews are seen in heaven (Mount Zion and before the throne with the four cherubim). The passage notes that they have been redeemed from mankind as the first fruits of God and the Lamb. The only way they could have gone to heaven is through dying. Rev 15 confirms this. Just before the bowls are unleashed, John sees those who have conquered the beast and its image and the number of its name standing beside the sea of glass with harps of God in their hands. Notice that this resembles the description of the great multitude found in heaven before the throne; however, those were "clothed in white robes, with palm branches in their hands," whereas these have harps in their hands:

> Then I saw another sign in heaven, great and amazing, seven angels with seven plagues, which are the last, for with them the wrath of God is finished.
>
> ² And I saw what appeared to be a sea of glass mingled with fire—and also those who had conquered the beast and its image and the number of its name, standing beside the sea of glass with harps of God in their hands. ³ And they sing the song of Moses, the servant of God, and the song of the Lamb, saying,
>
> "Great and amazing are your deeds,
>   O Lord God the Almighty!
> Just and true are your ways,
>   O King of the nations!
> ⁴ Who will not fear, O Lord, and glorify your name?

> For you alone are holy.
> All nations will come and worship you, for your righteous acts have been revealed."
>
> ⁵ After this I looked, and the sanctuary of the tent of witness in heaven was opened, ⁶ and out of the sanctuary came the seven angels with the seven plagues, clothed in pure, bright linen, with golden sashes around their chests. ⁷ And one of the four living creatures gave to the seven angels seven golden bowls full of the wrath of God who lives forever and ever, ⁸ and the sanctuary was filled with smoke from the glory of God and from his power, and no one could enter the sanctuary until the seven plagues of the seven angels were finished. (Rev 15:1–8)

The harps in their hands tie these to the 144,000 Jews and not to the great multitude previously found in heaven. Recall that when they are seen on Mount Zion with the Lamb, harps are heard in heaven:

> The voice I heard was like the sound of harpists playing on their harps, ³ and they were singing a new song before the throne and before the four living creatures and before the elders. No one could learn that song except the 144,000 who had been redeemed from the earth. (Rev 14:2–3)

Hence, these are redeemed from the earth before the bowls are poured out.

For three and a half years, the two witnesses had been preaching to the 144,000 Jews—essentially bringing them up to speed with the gospel of Jesus. At the end of their witnesses, the 144,000 Jews are ripe for redemption. Just the same way God allowed the antichrist to kill the two witnesses, he will allow the antichrist to kill the 144,000, and their souls will be received in heaven just like the souls of Christians who died during the great tribulation. The 144,000 are described as having conquered the antichrist (conquered the beast and its image and the number of its name). However, the book of Revelation seems to suggest that the only way to conquer the antichrist is for believers to be killed by the antichrist while proclaiming the testimony of Christ and God, just as the two witnesses were killed at the end of their mission:

> And they have conquered him by the blood of the Lamb and by the word of their testimony, for they loved not their lives even unto death. (Rev 12:11)

It is also possible that God may redeem the 144,000 Jews through another means. But the key message here is that the 144,000 will be taken out of the earth just before the seven bowls of the wrath of God are poured out on the earth.

To buttress this further, Dan 12 tends to suggest that towards the end of time and before the white throne Judgment, the Jews will be delivered from the torments they have been subjected to for a period covering 1,260 days:

> At that time shall arise Michael, the great prince who has charge of your people. And there shall be a time of trouble, such as never has been since there was a nation till that time. But at that time your people shall be delivered, everyone whose name shall be found written in the book. (Dan 12:1)

5.14. THE MESSAGES OF THE THREE ANGELS— CALL FOR THE ENDURANCE OF SAINTS

Then I saw another angel flying directly overhead, with an eternal gospel to proclaim to those who dwell on earth, to every nation and tribe and language and people. [7] And he said with a loud voice, "Fear God and give him glory, because the hour of his judgment has come, and worship him who made heaven and earth, the sea and the springs of water."

[8] Another angel, a second, followed, saying, "Fallen, fallen is Babylon the great, she who made all nations drink the wine of the passion of her sexual immorality."

[9] And another angel, a third, followed them, saying with a loud voice, "If anyone worships the beast and its image and receives a mark on his forehead or on his hand, [10] he also will drink the wine of God's wrath, poured full strength into the cup of his anger, and he will be tormented with fire and sulfur in the presence of the holy angels and in the presence of the Lamb. [11] And the smoke of their torment goes up forever and ever, and they have no rest, day or night, these worshipers of the beast and its image, and whoever receives the mark of its name."

[12] Here is a call for the endurance of the saints, those who keep the commandments of God and their faith in Jesus.

[13] And I heard a voice from heaven saying, "Write this: Blessed are the dead who die in the Lord from now on." "Blessed indeed," says the Spirit, "that they may rest from their labors, for their deeds follow them!" (Rev 14:6–13)

Although situated in Rev 14, the messages of the three angels will come on the heels of the sixth trumpet. Most likely the call is made just before the seventh trumpet is blown. In line with God's righteous stance, these are meant to warn the inhabitants of the world of what is about to come—the hour of God's judgment has come:

> Fear God and give him glory, because the hour of his judgment has come, and worship him who made heaven and earth, the sea and the springs of water. (Rev 14:7)

It is important to note here that the *hour* of his judgment is used. The seventh seal period is the period for God's wrath/judgment on the world, referred to as the *day* of his wrath:

> For the great day of their wrath has come, and who can stand? (Rev 6:17)

Hence, the "hour of his judgment" marks the specific part of this period of wrath when the judgment will climax—the seventh trumpet. The messages of the three angels are the final warning from God of the coming judgment against unbelievers. They outline key events that will take place at this time, such as the fall of Babylon and the judgment of those who worshipped the beast. The messages of the third angel specifically outline how those who worshipped the beast and its image will be punished, hence suggesting that they haven't yet received their judgment.

The saints are called to endure:

> Here is a call for the endurance of the saints, those who keep the commandments of God and their faith in Jesus. (Rev 14:12)

These saints being asked to endure must be the last of the Christians who are still on earth, because by this point the 144,000 have been redeemed from the earth (see §5.13), thus situating this event to occur just before the seventh trumpet.

5.15. THE HARVEST OF THE EARTH

> Then I looked, and behold, a white cloud, and seated on the cloud one like a son of man, with a golden crown on his head, and a sharp sickle in his hand. [15] And another angel came out of the temple, calling with a loud voice to him who sat on the cloud, "Put in your sickle, and reap, for the hour to reap has come, for the harvest of the earth is fully ripe." [16] So he who sat

on the cloud swung his sickle across the earth, and the earth was reaped. [17] Then another angel came out of the temple in heaven, and he too had a sharp sickle. [18] And another angel came out from the altar, the angel who has authority over the fire, and he called with a loud voice to the one who had the sharp sickle, "Put in your sickle and gather the clusters from the vine of the earth, for its grapes are ripe." [19] So the angel swung his sickle across the earth and gathered the grape harvest of the earth and threw it into the great winepress of the wrath of God. [20] And the winepress was trodden outside the city, and blood flowed from the winepress, as high as a horse's bridle, for 1,600 stadia. (Rev 14:14–20)

This passage is symbolic, more like a parable rather than an actual event. It is a parable that provides a summary of the events to come: believers will soon be gathered to where Christ will be establishing his kingdom on earth, and God will pour out his wrath on unbelievers.

Matthew 24:31 seems to point to this gathering of the elect:

Then will appear in heaven the sign of the Son of Man, and then all the tribes of the earth will mourn, and they will see the Son of Man coming on the clouds of heaven with power and great glory. [31] And he will send out his angels with a loud trumpet call, and they will gather his elect from the four winds, from one end of heaven to the other. (Matt 24:30–31)

The parable of the wheat and tares was pointing to this particular event, where the wheat represents believers still on earth, and the tares represent the unrepentant world:

He answered and said to them: "He who sows the good seed is the Son of Man. [38] The field is the world, the good seeds are the sons of the kingdom, but the tares are the sons of the wicked one. [39] The enemy who sowed them is the devil, the harvest is the end of the age, and the reapers are the angels. [40] Therefore as the tares are gathered and burned in the fire, so it will be at the end of this age. [41] The Son of Man will send out His angels, and they will gather out of His kingdom all things that offend, and those who practice lawlessness, [42] and will cast them into the furnace of fire. There will be wailing and gnashing of teeth. [43] Then the righteous will shine forth as the sun in the kingdom of their Father. He who has ears to hear, let him hear! (Matt 13:37–44)

It is pertinent to note here that there is an almost immediate action against unbelievers as soon as the saints are gathered. As soon as the believers are gathered, angels are sent to gather unbelievers to face God's wrath:

> Then another angel came out of the temple in heaven, and he too had a sharp sickle. [18] And another angel came out from the altar, the angel who has authority over the fire, and he called with a loud voice to the one who had the sharp sickle, "Put in your sickle and gather the clusters from the vine of the earth, for its grapes are ripe." [19] So the angel swung his sickle across the earth and gathered the grape harvest of the earth and threw it into the great winepress of the wrath of God. (Rev 14:17-19)

This seems to align with the events foretold by Jesus Christ in Luke 17, where devastation will come upon the earth as soon as the saints are taken out of the stage:

> Just as it was in the days of Noah, so will it be in the days of the Son of Man. [27] They were eating and drinking and marrying and being given in marriage, until the day when Noah entered the ark, and the flood came and destroyed them all. [28] Likewise, just as it was in the days of Lot—they were eating and drinking, buying and selling, planting and building, [29] but on the day when Lot went out from Sodom, fire and sulfur rained from heaven and destroyed them all— [30] so will it be on the day when the Son of Man is revealed. [31] On that day, let the one who is on the housetop, with his goods in the house, not come down to take them away, and likewise let the one who is in the field not turn back. [32] Remember Lot's wife. [33] Whoever seeks to preserve his life will lose it, but whoever loses his life will keep it. [34] I tell you, in that night there will be two in one bed. One will be taken and the other left. [35] There will be two women grinding together. One will be taken and the other left." [37] And they said to him, "Where, Lord?" He said to them, "Where the corpse is, there the vultures will gather." (Luke 17:26-37)

5.16. WERE THERE CHRISTIANS ON EARTH DURING THE SEVENTH TRUMPET PERIOD?

There are pointers in the Bible that seem to suggest that some followers of Christ will manage to evade the persecution of the antichrist and be alive till Christ returns to earth:

> Brother will deliver brother over to death, and the father his child, and children will rise against parents and have them put to death, [22] and you will be hated by all for my name's sake. But the one who endures to the end will be saved. [23] When they persecute you in one town, flee to the next, for truly, I say to you, you will not have gone through all the towns of Israel before the Son of Man comes. (Matt 10:21–23)

The above passage may be referring to both Christians and the 144,000 Jews who will be on earth until they are harvested out of the earth—the first fruits from earth—just before Christ arrives on earth. Paul in his First Letter to Thessalonians hinted at this and provided more clarity that there will be Christians on earth up to the time Christ will come on earth:

> For the Lord himself will descend from heaven with a cry of command, with the voice of an archangel, and with the sound of the trumpet of God. And the dead in Christ will rise first. [17] *Then we who are alive, who are left*, will be caught up together with them in the clouds to meet the Lord in the air, and so we will always be with the Lord. (1 Thess 4:16–17)

Notice here that Paul says: "Then we who are alive, who are left . . ." The phrase "who are left" suggests that something has happened to others belonging to the same group. Others have either died or been taken away. Considering that many Christians will have been killed by the antichrist (the martyrs of the great tribulation), it is appropriate to consider those who are still on earth as those who are left. This could also cover the fact that the 144,000 Jews have been redeemed from earth as the first fruits, thus leaving behind Christians who will still be living on earth when Christ appears to all mankind (see §6.7).

To buttress this, the event narrated in Rev 14 is happening at the heels of the demise of the two witnesses (which is part of the events of the sixth trumpet) and just before the seven bowls are unleashed on the earth (seventh trumpet). Furthermore, part of the messages of the three angels is directed at believers who are still on earth, admonishing them not to succumb and take the mark of the beast and asking them to continue to endure:

> And another angel, a third, followed them, saying with a loud voice, "If anyone worships the beast and its image and receives a mark on his forehead or on his hand, [10] he also will drink the wine of God's wrath, poured full strength into the cup of his anger, and he will be tormented with fire and sulfur in the presence of the holy angels and in the presence of the Lamb. [11] And the smoke of their torment goes up forever and ever, and they have

no rest, day or night, these worshipers of the beast and its image, and whoever receives the mark of its name."

¹² Here is a call for the endurance of the saints, those who keep the commandments of God and their faith in Jesus. (Rev 14:9–13)

Thus, at this point (when the messages are delivered), there are the following categories of people on earth: Christians (some in hiding within the secular world, those still held in various prisons across the world, and others possibly being nourished in the "wilderness" on earth but out of reach of the antichrist) and the rest of humanity still operating within the secular world (within the reach of the antichrist).

Furthermore, Christ hinted that during the events of the end-time, not all Christians will be killed. Some Christians will be killed, and others who are not killed will have to endure the hardship and persecution of the time:

> You will be delivered up even by parents and brothers and relatives and friends, and *some of you they will put to death.* ¹⁷ *You will be hated by all for my name's sake.* ¹⁸ *But not a hair of your head will perish.* ¹⁹ *By your endurance you will gain your lives.* (Luke 21:16–19)

Hence, only *some* and not all Christians will be put to death!

Perhaps Christians still on earth are severally admonished to endure because the events that God will unleash on the earth may also affect them.

6

The Seventh Trumpet: The Last Trump

6.1. PRELUDE TO THE SEVENTH TRUMPET

Then I saw another mighty angel coming down from heaven, wrapped in a cloud, with a rainbow over his head, and his face was like the sun, and his legs like pillars of fire. ² He had a little scroll open in his hand. And he set his right foot on the sea, and his left foot on the land, ³ and called out with a loud voice, like a lion roaring. When he called out, the seven thunders sounded. ⁴ And when the seven thunders had sounded, I was about to write, but I heard a voice from heaven saying, "Seal up what the seven thunders have said, and do not write it down." ⁵ And the angel whom I saw standing on the sea and on the land raised his right hand to heaven ⁶ and swore by him who lives forever and ever, who created heaven and what is in it, the earth and what is in it, and the sea and what is in it, that there would be no more delay, ⁷ *but that in the days of the trumpet call to be sounded by the seventh angel, the mystery of God would be fulfilled*, just as he announced to his servants the prophets.

⁸ Then the voice that I had heard from heaven spoke to me again, saying, "Go, take the scroll that is open in the hand of the angel who is standing on the sea and on the land." ⁹ So I went to the angel and told him to give me the little scroll. And he said to me, "Take and eat it; it will make your stomach bitter, but in your mouth it will be sweet as honey." ¹⁰ And I took the little scroll from the hand of the angel and ate it. It was sweet as honey

> in my mouth, but when I had eaten it my stomach was made bitter. [11] And I was told, "You must again prophesy about many peoples and nations and languages and kings." (Rev 10:1–11)

Although placed at Rev 10, chronologically speaking, this event of "a mighty angel coming down from heaven, wrapped in a cloud, with a rainbow over his head," seems to be a prelude of the events of the seventh trumpet and probably happens at the end of events of the sixth trumpet. The purpose is to proclaim that the dreadful moment is about to come:

> And swore by him who lives forever and ever, who created heaven and what is in it, the earth and what is in it, and the sea and what is in it, that there would be no more delay, *but that in the days of the trumpet call to be sounded by the seventh angel, the mystery of God would be fulfilled,* just as he announced to his servants the prophets. (Rev 10:6–7)

God in his righteousness always adheres to the cosmic/divine law that expects that before any action is carried out on earth, it must be proclaimed to the people. Hence, every key stage of the end-time is announced to humanity.

6.2. THE SEVENTH TRUMPET (THIRD WOE— WRAPPING UP GOD'S JUDGMENT)

> Then the seventh angel blew his trumpet, and there were loud voices in heaven, saying, "The kingdom of the world has become the kingdom of our Lord and of his Christ, and he shall reign forever and ever." [16] And the twenty-four elders who sit on their thrones before God fell on their faces and worshiped God, [17] saying,
> "We give thanks to you, Lord God Almighty, who is and who was, for you have taken your great." (Rev 11:15–17)

The events of the seventh trumpet begin with proclamation from heavenly beings exalting God and declaring that the earthly kingdom has finally become the kingdom of God. The whole essence of the events of the revelation is geared towards this end—to reclaim control of the world from Satan and to make it God's kingdom. Satan stole the control of the earthly kingdom from Adam at Eden, which disrupted God's plans for humans. The first coming of Christ (his death on the cross and resurrection) legally removed every authority Satan had on earth:

THE SEVENTH TRUMPET: THE LAST TRUMP 123

Then Jesus came to them and said, "*All authority in heaven and on earth has been given to me.*" (Matt 28:18)

"I have told you these things, so that in me you may have peace. In this world you will have trouble. But take heart! *I have overcome the world.*" (John 16:33)

That power is the same as the mighty strength [20] he exerted when he raised Christ from the dead and *seated him at his right hand in the heavenly realms,* [21] *far above all rule and authority, power and dominion, and every name that is invoked, not only in the present age but also in the one to come.* [22] And God placed all things under his feet and appointed him to be head over everything for the church, [23] which is his body, the fullness of him who fills everything in every way. (Eph 1:19–23).

Christ's second coming is to complete the process—capturing Satan and imprisoning him. Hence, the blowing of the seventh trumpet launches a momentous stage in the end-time agenda.

It encompasses the following events:

- Punishment/wrath of God on the earth—*the nations raged, but your wrath came*
- Judgment of the dead—*time for the dead to be judged*
- Rewarding of God's servants, prophets, and saints, and those who fear God's name—*for rewarding your servants*
- Destruction of the enemies of God, who destroyed the earth—*and for destroying the destroyers of the earth.* (Rev 11:18)

The key event of the seventh trumpet is the unleashing of the seven bowls of wrath on the earth and its inhabitants. For every bowl poured, some events follow. Events following the pouring out of the contents of each bowl on the earth mark the final punishment of God against Satan and his followers, which are unleashed in stages with increasing intensity. At each step, a section of the earth is affected, and this is ramped up until the battle at Armageddon.

6.3. THE SEVEN PLAGUES (THE UNLEASHING OF THE SEVEN BOWLS OF GOD'S WRATH)

> Then I saw another sign in heaven, great and amazing, seven angels with seven plagues, which are the last, for with them the wrath of God is finished. (Rev 15:1)

> After this I looked, and the sanctuary of the tent of witness in heaven was opened, ⁶ and out of the sanctuary came the seven angels with the seven plagues, clothed in pure, bright linen, with golden sashes around their chests. ⁷ And one of the four living creatures gave to the seven angels seven golden bowls full of the wrath of God who lives forever and ever, ⁸ and the sanctuary was filled with smoke from the glory of God and from his power, and no one could enter the sanctuary until the seven plagues of the seven angels were finished. (Rev 15:5–8)

Similar to what happened in the seventh seal (nested sequence of events), the blowing of the seventh trumpet leads to a series of seven new distinct events known as the seven bowls of God's wrath or seven plagues. The plagues are essentially a wrapping up of God's judgment on earth, hence this is more devastating than what had happened in the previous trumpets. As a matter of fact, the events of the previous trumpet foreshadowed the seven bowls events.

6.3.1 The First Bowl of God's Wrath—Sores on Those with the Mark of the Beast

> Then I heard a loud voice from the temple telling the seven angels, "Go and pour out on the earth the seven bowls of the wrath of God."
> ² So the first angel went and poured out his bowl on the earth, and harmful and painful sores came upon the people who bore the mark of the beast and worshiped its image. (Rev 16:1–2)

The event associated with the pouring out of the contents of the first bowl is targeted at those who have taken the mark of the beast. It may be that something will make the technology behind the mark malfunction and lead to a sore (disease) on those who have it. One thing that jumps out here is that at this time there may be some people who did not take the mark, hence it is specified that only those with the mark will be affected by this plague.

6.3.2 The Second Bowl—Contamination of the Sea and Destruction of Marine Life

> The second angel poured out his bowl into the sea, and it became like the blood of a corpse, and every living thing died that was in the sea. (Rev 16:3).

When the second bowl is unleashed on the earth, all living creatures in the sea will be annihilated, hence, the sea will change to blood. This wrath (second bowl) is almost like the wrath against marine lives in the second trumpet (§5.6); however, the key difference is whereas one-third of the marine environment is impacted in the former, all marine lives are affected in the latter (second bowl). Hence, this is a more intense and devastating plague than the earth has experienced. Also, the causative agent used in the second trumpet is "something like a great mountain, burning with fire," whereas the content of the bowl is poured out into the sea. This differentiates both events.

6.3.3 The Third Bowl—Contamination of Fresh Water

> The third angel poured out his bowl into the rivers and the springs of water, and they became blood. ⁵ And I heard the angel in charge of the waters say,
> "Just are you, O Holy One, who is and who was, for you brought these judgments. ⁶ For they have shed the blood of saints and prophets, and you have given them blood to drink. It is what they deserve!"
> ⁷ And I heard the altar saying, "Yes, Lord God the Almighty, true and just are your judgments!" (Rev 16:4–7)

The wrath of the third bowl is targeting fresh water of the world (just like the third trumpet does). The purpose is to contaminate the waters as a way of punishing inhabitants of the earth:

> For they have shed the blood of saints and prophets, and you have given them blood to drink. (Rev 16:6)

6.3.4 The Fourth Bowl—Unleashing of Severe Solar Flares on Humanity

> The fourth angel poured out his bowl on the sun, and it was allowed to scorch people with fire. [9] They were scorched by the fierce heat, and they cursed the name of God who had power over these plagues. They did not repent and give him glory. (Rev 16:8–9)

The wrath of the fourth bowl is directly on an astronomic body and indirectly on humans. The wrath poured on this entity causes it to malfunction and became an agent of torment targeting humans. Hence, in this wrath, the instrument of torment is the sun, via severe solar flare that is scorching people with heat and fire. Despite all this, the people are not repenting. What could be stopping them from repenting? Stubbornness or media propaganda/rationalization by scientists that these are impacts of climate change?

6.3.5 The Fifth Bowl—Wrath against the Throne of the Beast

> The fifth angel poured out his bowl on the throne of the beast, and its kingdom was plunged into darkness. People gnawed their tongues in anguish [11] and cursed the God of heaven for their pain and sores. They did not repent of their deeds. (Rev 16:10–11)

The fifth bowl is targeted at destroying the seat of power of the beast. This will probably destroy all technologies, including AI surveillance systems and smart and big data infrastructures that the beast will have been using to run its government and put the world in check. Expectedly, the destruction of the seat of power of the beast will plunge the antichrist system into disarray and darkness. It should be noted that people are still experiencing pains from the sores that appeared when the first bowl was poured out. The location of the seat of power of the antichrist is not explicitly stated in Revelation. However, going by the book of Daniel, speculations as to where this might be can be glimpsed:

> And he shall pitch his palatial tents between the sea and the glorious holy mountain. (Dan 11:45)

6.3.6 The Sixth Bowl—Drying up of the River Euphrates and Preparation for the Battle of Armageddon

> The sixth angel poured out his bowl on the great river Euphrates, and its water was dried up, to prepare the way for the kings from the east. [13] And I saw, coming out of the mouth of the dragon and out of the mouth of the beast and out of the mouth of the false prophet, three unclean spirits like frogs. [14] For they are demonic spirits, performing signs, who go abroad to the kings of the whole world, to assemble them for battle on the great day of God the Almighty. [15] ("Behold, I am coming like a thief! Blessed is the one who stays awake, keeping his garments on, that he may not go about naked and be seen exposed!") [16] And they assembled them at the place that in Hebrew is called Armageddon (Rev 16:12–16)

The key event of the sixth bowl is the drying up of the Euphrates River. At this point, having experienced the torments of the previous plagues, it has become clear to Satan of what is coming. Hence, this is the point he starts to prepare for war against the armies of God, who are coming towards the earth with Jesus, for the final takeover of the world. Satan (the dragon), the antichrist (the first beast), and the false prophet (the second beast) synergize their efforts to convince world leaders to join forces with them. The drying up of the Euphrates will facilitate the movement of troops from the eastern flanks of the world (east of Israel/Jerusalem). The Euphrates runs across Iraq. East of Euphrates lie major countries such as Iran, China, Afghanistan, Pakistan, and India. Hence, this implies that troops from Iran, China, and other countries might join troops from other countries such as those from Iraq, Saudi Arabia, Jordan, Syria, Turkey, Egypt, Libya, etc. at Armageddon, in preparation for the great battle.

Christians are reminded here that the long-awaited sudden coming of Christ and his army like a thief in the night is imminent:

> [15] ("Behold, I am coming like a thief! Blessed is the one who stays awake, keeping his garments on, that he may not go about naked and be seen exposed!"). (Rev 16:15)

> Therefore, stay awake, for you do not know on what day your Lord is coming. [43] But know this, that if the master of the house had known in what part of the night the thief was coming, he would have stayed awake and would not have let his house be broken into. [44] Therefore you also must be ready, for the Son of Man is coming at an hour you do not expect. (Matt 24:42–44)

> For you yourselves are fully aware that the day of the Lord will come like a thief in the night. ³ While people are saying, "There is peace and security," then sudden destruction will come upon them as labor pains come upon a pregnant woman, and they will not escape. ⁴ But you are not in darkness, brothers, for that day to surprise you like a thief. ⁵ For you are all children of light, children of the day. We are not of the night or of the darkness. (1 Thess 5:2–4)

6.3.7 The Seventh Bowl—Great Earthquake, Destruction of World Cities

> The seventh angel poured out his bowl into the air, and a loud voice came out of the temple, from the throne, saying, "It is done!" ¹⁸ And there were flashes of lightning, rumblings, peals of thunder, and a great earthquake such as there had never been since man was on the earth, so great was that earthquake. ¹⁹ The great city was split into three parts, and the cities of the nations fell, and God remembered Babylon the great, to make her drain the cup of the wine of the fury of his wrath. ²⁰ And every island fled away, and no mountains were to be found. ²¹ And great hailstones, about one hundred pounds each, fell from heaven on people; and they cursed God for the plague of the hail, because the plague was so severe. (Rev 16:17–21)

In this last plague the atmosphere is targeted. Thus, every aspect of the earth—terrestrial (earth), marine (water), astronomic (fire), and atmospheric (air)—environments are each judged. This is a slow but definite shutdown of the earth, preparing it for the final takeover by Jesus Christ and the armies of God.

The key event of this plague is a great earthquake with intensity that has never been experienced before, hitting the earth. This causes the great city (most likely Jerusalem) to split into three parts, major cities across the world fall ("cities of the nations fell"), and Babylon falls ("and God remembered Babylon the great, to make her drain the cup of the wine of the fury of his wrath"). This earthquake probably shakes mountains and possibly reaches the seabed, thus causing massive tsunamis across the world that obliterate islands ("And every island fled away, and no mountains were to be found"). This event culminates in massive hailstones falling on earth and killing people ("And great hailstones, about one hundred pounds each, fell from heaven on people; and they cursed God for the plague of the hail, because the plague was so severe").

6.3.8. The Great Prostitute and the Beast

Then one of the seven angels who had the seven bowls came and said to me, "Come, I will show you the judgment of the great prostitute who is seated on many waters, [2] with whom the kings of the earth have committed sexual immorality, and with the wine of whose sexual immorality the dwellers on earth have become drunk." [3] And he carried me away in the Spirit into a wilderness, and I saw a woman sitting on a scarlet beast that was full of blasphemous names, and it had seven heads and ten horns. [4] The woman was arrayed in purple and scarlet, and adorned with gold and jewels and pearls, holding in her hand a golden cup full of abominations and the impurities of her sexual immorality. [5] And on her forehead was written a name of mystery: "Babylon the great, mother of prostitutes and of earth's abominations." [6] And I saw the woman, drunk with the blood of the saints, the blood of the martyrs of Jesus.

When I saw her, I marveled greatly. [7] But the angel said to me, "Why do you marvel? I will tell you the mystery of the woman, and of the beast with seven heads and ten horns that carries her. [8] The beast that you saw was, and is not, and is about to rise from the bottomless pit and go to destruction. And the dwellers on earth whose names have not been written in the book of life from the foundation of the world will marvel to see the beast, because it was and is not and is to come. [9] This calls for a mind with wisdom: the seven heads are seven mountains on which the woman is seated; [10] they are also seven kings, five of whom have fallen, one is, the other has not yet come, and when he does come he must remain only a little while. [11] As for the beast that was and is not, it is an eighth but it belongs to the seven, and it goes to destruction. [12] And the ten horns that you saw are ten kings who have not yet received royal power, but they are to receive authority as kings for one hour, together with the beast. [13] These are of one mind, and they hand over their power and authority to the beast. [14] They will make war on the Lamb, and the Lamb will conquer them, for he is Lord of lords and King of kings, and those with him are called and chosen and faithful."

¹⁵ And the angel said to me, "The waters that you saw, where the prostitute is seated, are peoples and multitudes and nations and languages. ¹⁶ And the ten horns that you saw, they and the beast will hate the prostitute. They will make her desolate and naked, and devour her flesh and burn her up with fire, ¹⁷ for God has put it into their hearts to carry out his purpose by being of one mind and handing over their royal power to the beast, until the words of God are fulfilled. ¹⁸ And the woman that you saw is the great city that has dominion over the kings of the earth." (Rev 17:1–18)

The woman sitting on the scarlet beast is the great prostitute who is seated on many waters. She is also referred to as Babylon the great. The woman is the spiritual representation of a city:

> And he carried me away in the Spirit into a wilderness, and I saw a woman sitting on a scarlet beast that was full of blasphemous names. (Rev 17:3)

This city is possibly where the antichrist's government will be headquartered or where he has a great influence. The phrase "sitting on many waters" may mean control over many countries/people across the world. Thus, the waters upon which the woman sits ("are peoples and multitudes and nations and languages"), which points to the fact that the influence of the woman cuts across many countries and people:

> And the woman that you saw is the great city that has dominion over the kings of the earth." (Rev 17:18)

This is not the first time that God has symbolically represented a city with a woman. In the book of Ezekiel, Samaria and Jerusalem were represented as women:

> The word of the LORD came to me: ² "Son of man, there were two women, the daughters of one mother. ³ They played the whore in Egypt; they played the whore in their youth; there their breasts were pressed and their virgin bosoms handled. ⁴ Oholah was the name of the elder and Oholibah the name of her sister. They became mine, and they bore sons and daughters. As for their names, Oholah is Samaria, and Oholibah is Jerusalem. (Ezek 23:1–4)

This great prostitute is also described as having committed sexual immorality with the kings of the earth:

> "Come, I will show you the judgment of the great prostitute who is seated on many waters, ² with whom the kings of the earth

have committed sexual immorality, and with the wine of whose sexual immorality the dwellers on earth have become drunk." (Rev 17:1–2)

The Bible contains various instances where God referred to Israel/Judah as harlots or prostitutes who defiled themselves with kings and commanders of other nations (the book of Hosea, Ezek 23, etc.). God used this to symbolize the behaviour of Israelites turning away from him and worshipping the gods of other nations. Hence, it wouldn't be surprising to see here that the great prostitute could be a nation/city like Jerusalem that turned away from God to embrace the antichrist. Although the prophecies of Ezek 23 and 24 were fulfilled at the time, they might also be referring to this final destruction of Jerusalem. A key part of the eschatological events is the invasion of Jerusalem by the antichrist to declare himself as God in the temple of God (the abomination of desolation, which Jesus Christ admonished his followers to watch out for as a significant marker of the events of the end-time):

> He shall turn back and pay attention to those who forsake the holy covenant. [31] Forces from him shall appear and profane the temple and fortress, and shall take away the regular burnt offering. And they shall set up the abomination that makes desolate. [32] He shall seduce with flattery those who violate the covenant, but the people who know their God shall stand firm and take action. (Dan 11:30–32)

Unfortunately, many Jews who rejected Jesus Christ will embrace the antichrist as the messiah:

> "I have come in my Father's name, and you do not receive me. If another comes in his own name, you will receive him." (John 5:43)

> And the king shall do as he wills. He shall exalt himself and magnify himself above every god, and shall speak astonishing things against the God of gods. He shall prosper till the indignation is accomplished; for what is decreed shall be done. (Dan 11:36)

God will view this action of Jews turning away from him to embrace the antichrist as prostitution/harlotry, considering his preestablished precepts and standards, which he revealed through the ancient prophets. John marveled at seeing the woman riding the beast, which is an indication that he was shocked to recognize Jerusalem and her relationship with the beast.

The scarlet beast is different from the first beast (antichrist) seen in Rev 13 (see §4.5), even though they seem to have some similarities such as seven heads and ten horns. However, something that jumps out here is that unlike the first beast, the scarlet beast has no diadem/crown. Secondly, the first beast rises from the sea, whereas the scarlet beast rises from the bottomless pit:

> The beast that you saw was, and is not, and is about to rise from the bottomless pit and go to destruction. And the dwellers on earth whose names have not been written in the book of life from the foundation of the world will marvel to see the beast, because it was and is not and is to come. (Rev 17:8)

Whereas the first beast represents an individual, the scarlet beast represents an old system of government/kingdom/empire that has largely disappeared, which will reemerge:

> As for the beast that was and is not, it is an eighth but it belongs to the seven, and it goes to destruction. (Rev 17:11)

This could possibly be the reemergence of the Ottoman or Roman Empire or a combination of both. Recall the kingdom whose feet were "partly of iron and partly of clay" in Nebuchadnezzar's dream:

> "You saw, O king, and behold, a great image. This image, mighty and of exceeding brightness, stood before you, and its appearance was frightening. [32] The head of this image was of fine gold, its chest and arms of silver, its middle and thighs of bronze, [33] its legs of iron, its feet partly of iron and partly of clay. [34] As you looked, a stone was cut out by no human hand, and it struck the image on its feet of iron and clay, and broke them in pieces. [35] Then the iron, the clay, the bronze, the silver, and the gold, all together were broken in pieces, and became like the chaff of the summer threshing floors; and the wind carried them away, so that not a trace of them could be found. But the stone that struck the image became a great mountain and filled the whole earth. (Dan 2:31–35)

It is instructive to note here that the beast is scarlet-colored, the same color as the Ottoman Empire flag, which Turkey is currently using. The Roman Empire flag could also be considered scarlet; however, it is no longer in use today, unlike the Ottoman Empire's, which is being used by Turkey, a country that could be considered a mix of Western democracy and Islamic tyranny ("feet partly of iron and partly of clay"). It could be that that the new system will emerge from present-day Turkey. It is imperative to note that at a point, the Roman Empire became a divided empire with two capitals at Rome and Constantinople (present-day Istanbul—see box 6.1). If Rome was the iron kingdom in Nebuchadnezzar's dream ("its legs of iron"), it perfectly makes sense that this kingdom was depicted with two legs, that is, two parts of the same. This kingdom was eventually whittled down and gave way to the next empire that was a mix of clay and iron ("its feet partly of iron and partly of clay"). Hence, it became fragile to this day.

Box 6.1: Division of the Roman Empire

> The Roman Empire was first divided into two parts (eastern and western halves) in 285 CE by Emperor Diocletian. However, Emperor Constantine in 330 CE moved the capital of the Roman Empire to Byzantium (Constantinople). It was from the Byzantine Empire that the Ottoman Empire emerged after 1453. The Western Roman Empire in Rome was replaced with the Holy Roman Empire from 800 to 1806.

It is apparent from the angel's interpretation of the mystery that the seven heads of the beast are a double symbol used to represent two different aspects of the antichrist/beast system. Thus, the caution by the angel that "this calls for a mind with wisdom" (Rev 17:9).

Firstly, the seven heads of the beast represent seven mountains/blocks of countries or regions that the woman sits upon or controls. Thus, the beast system may be run through the division of its sphere of influence into seven major blocks referred to as mountains. These blocks will be controlled (seated upon) from the city (the mysterious Babylon represented by the great prostitute):

> The seven heads are seven mountains on which the woman is seated. (Rev 17:9)

Second, the seven heads were also used to link up the beast system to previous empires of significance. Thus, the angel says that the seven heads also represent seven kings/empires, five of which have fallen (disappeared), one of which exists, and one of which will come and will remain briefly:

> They are also seven kings, five of whom have fallen, one is, the other has not yet come, and when he does come he must remain only a little while.[11] As for the beast that was and is not, it is an eighth but it belongs to the seven, and it goes to destruction. (Rev 17:10–11)

Assuming the five kings/kingdoms are referring to the five kingdoms represented in Nebuchadnezzar's dream (ending with the Ottoman Empire), it may imply that the sixth might be the current Turkish government, which is an offshoot of the Ottoman Empire ("the one that is"). The seventh kingdom could be a reemergence of the Ottoman Empire (consisting of

Turkey and other nations), towards the time of the end ("the other that has not come"), and from this the eighth kingdom that will be headed by the antichrist will emerge. The eighth kingdom could be the final confederation of nations that the antichrist and false prophet will forge to combat Christ's army at the battle of Armageddon:

> And I saw, coming out of the mouth of the dragon and out of the mouth of the beast and out of the mouth of the false prophet, three unclean spirits like frogs. ¹⁴ For they are demonic spirits, performing signs, who go abroad to the kings of the whole world, to assemble them for battle on the great day of God the Almighty. (Rev 16:13–14)

> And I saw the beast and the kings of the earth with their armies gathered to make war against him who was sitting on the horse and against his army. (Rev 19:19)

Hence, this kingdom/confederation of nations does not last long—lasting only for an hour, as it rises to go into destruction at Armageddon:

> As for the beast that was and is not, it is an eighth but it belongs to the seven, and it goes to destruction. ¹² And the ten horns that you saw are ten kings who have not yet received royal power, but they are to receive authority as kings for one hour, together with the beast. ¹³ These are of one mind, and they hand over their power and authority to the beast. ¹⁴ They will make war on the Lamb, and the Lamb will conquer them, for he is Lord of lords and King of kings, and those with him are called and chosen and faithful. (Rev 17:11–14)

This tends to tally with the events of Dan 11, which narrated the struggles between various kings from the Babylonian time through the Greco-Roman Empire to the time that the antichrist finally emerged and took power (see §3.5.2).

One thing to note here is that the angel seems to be interpreting the scarlet beast as a kingdom/system of government (of the antichrist) as well as an individual (antichrist). This double meaning should not be surprising, considering it was deployed earlier for the seven heads of the beast. This becomes clearer when the angel is interpreting the meaning of the horns as ten kings ("the ten horns are ten kings yet to receive their powers"). The fact that these ten horns are kings who have not received their powers separates the ten kings from any king of previous empires/kingdoms. These are kings who will emerge towards the last phase of the end-time. They will rise to become kings at the same time the antichrist is also rising. However, they will

THE SEVENTH TRUMPET: THE LAST TRUMP 135

eventually form an alliance with the antichrist and hand over to him their power, either by deceit or coercion. This handover of power will perhaps happen just before the battle of Armageddon. "They will make war on the Lamb" points to the battle of Armageddon.

> And the ten horns that you saw are ten kings who have not yet received royal power, but they are to receive authority as kings for one hour, together with the beast. [13] These are of one mind, and they hand over their power and authority to the beast. [14] They will make war on the Lamb, and the Lamb will conquer them, for he is Lord of lords and King of kings, and those with him are called and chosen and faithful. (Rev 17:12–14)

Thus, it can be concluded that the scarlet beast is partly referring to the government/system that is facilitating/powering the activities of Babylon the great, as well as the antichrist himself who controls that system. It is possible that this beast is the same beast that killed the two witnesses:

> And when they have finished their testimony, the beast that rises from the bottomless pit will make war on them and conquer them and kill them, and their dead bodies will lie in the street of the great city that symbolically is called Sodom and Egypt, where their Lord was crucified. (Rev 11:7–8)

Finally, another hint that the woman (great prostitute) was used to depict Jerusalem is the fact that the woman is hated by the beast and the ten kings, hence, the reason the beast and ten kings will devour it. It is possible that the antichrist will delight to make Jerusalem, the darling of God, its headquarters (perhaps religious headquarters) or a key city for his government. This may be the motivation to invade Jerusalem. Based on the book of Daniel, the antichrist will defile/trample the temple of God in Jerusalem ("abomination of desolation"). The army of antichrist, composed mainly of Middle Eastern countries who hate Israel, will surely delight in destroying Jerusalem:

> And the angel said to me, "The waters that you saw, where the prostitute is seated, are peoples and multitudes and nations and languages. [16] And the ten horns that you saw, they and the beast will hate the prostitute. *They will make her desolate and naked, and devour her flesh and burn her up with fire.*" (Rev 17:15–16)

This might be what is being hinted at when the seventh bowl is poured out and the great city split into three parts, followed by a remark that God remembers Babylon the great:

The great city was split into three parts, and the cities of the nations fell, and God remembered Babylon the great, to make her drain the cup of the wine of the fury of his wrath. (Rev 16:19)

6.3.9. The Fall of Babylon

After this I saw another angel coming down from heaven, having great authority, and the earth was made bright with his glory. ² And he called out with a mighty voice,
"Fallen, fallen is Babylon the great!
 She has become a dwelling place for demons,
a haunt for every unclean spirit,
 a haunt for every unclean bird,
 a haunt for every unclean and detestable beast.
³ For all nations have drunk
 the wine of the passion of her sexual immorality,
and the kings of the earth have committed immorality with her,
 and the merchants of the earth have grown rich from the power of her luxurious living."
⁴ Then I heard another voice from heaven saying,
"Come out of her, my people,
 lest you take part in her sins,
lest you share in her plagues;
⁵ for her sins are heaped high as heaven,
 and God has remembered her iniquities.
⁶ Pay her back as she herself has paid back others,
 and repay her double for her deeds;
 mix a double portion for her in the cup she mixed.
⁷ As she glorified herself and lived in luxury,
 so give her a like measure of torment and mourning,
since in her heart she says,
 'I sit as a queen,
I am no widow,
 and mourning I shall never see.'
⁸ For this reason her plagues will come in a single day,
 death and mourning and famine,
and she will be burned up with fire;
 for mighty is the Lord God who has judged her."
⁹ And the kings of the earth, who committed sexual immorality and lived in luxury with her, will weep and wail over

her when they see the smoke of her burning. [10] They will stand far off, in fear of her torment, and say,

"Alas! Alas! You great city,
  you mighty city, Babylon!
 For in a single hour your judgment has come."

[11] And the merchants of the earth weep and mourn for her, since no one buys their cargo anymore, [12] cargo of gold, silver, jewels, pearls, fine linen, purple cloth, silk, scarlet cloth, all kinds of scented wood, all kinds of articles of ivory, all kinds of articles of costly wood, bronze, iron and marble, [13] cinnamon, spice, incense, myrrh, frankincense, wine, oil, fine flour, wheat, cattle and sheep, horses and chariots, and slaves, that is, human souls.

[14] "The fruit for which your soul longed
  has gone from you,
 and all your delicacies and your splendors
  are lost to you,
  never to be found again!"

[15] The merchants of these wares, who gained wealth from her, will stand far off, in fear of her torment, weeping and mourning aloud,

[16] "Alas, alas, for the great city
  that was clothed in fine linen,
   in purple and scarlet,
  adorned with gold,
   with jewels, and with pearls!
[17] For in a single hour all this wealth has been laid waste."

And all shipmasters and seafaring men, sailors and all whose trade is on the sea, stood far off [18] and cried out as they saw the smoke of her burning,

"What city was like the great city?"

[19] And they threw dust on their heads as they wept and mourned, crying out,

"Alas, alas, for the great city
  where all who had ships at sea
  grew rich by her wealth!
 For in a single hour she has been laid waste.
[20] Rejoice over her, O heaven,
   and you saints and apostles and prophets,
  for God has given judgment for you against her!"

[21] Then a mighty angel took up a stone like a great millstone and threw it into the sea, saying,

"So will Babylon the great city be thrown down with violence,

and will be found no more;
^{22} and the sound of harpists and musicians, of flute players and trumpeters,
will be heard in you no more,
and a craftsman of any craft
will be found in you no more,
and the sound of the mill
will be heard in you no more,
^{23} and the light of a lamp
will shine in you no more,
and the voice of bridegroom and bride
will be heard in you no more,
for your merchants were the great ones of the earth,
and all nations were deceived by your sorcery.
^{24} And in her was found the blood of prophets and of saints,
and of all who have been slain on earth." (Rev 18:1–24)

The declaration that Babylon has become a dwelling place for demons suggests that the city had not been that way before. Something happened to it that turned such a great city into a demon-infested city:

> Fallen, fallen is Babylon the great! She has become a dwelling place for demons, a haunt for every unclean spirit, a haunt for every unclean bird, a haunt for every unclean and detestable beast. (Rev 18:2)

In terms of the timing of this event, Babylon may fall (be destroyed) soon after the seventh bowl is poured out. Recalling the message of the three angels in Rev 14 (§5.13), the messages could be seen as outlining the sequence of events that will happen soon after the 144,000 Jews are harvested from the earth (§5.14). The first angel's message focuses on God's judgment (the seven bowls of wrath):

> Fear God and give him glory, because the hour of his judgment has come, and worship him who made heaven and earth, the sea and the springs of water. (Rev 14:7)

The second angel's message focuses on the fall of Babylon:

> Fallen, fallen is Babylon the great, she who made all nations drink the wine of the passion of her sexual immorality. (Rev 14:8)

The third angel's message focuses on the battle of Armageddon and what will happen to those who worship the beast and take the mark:

THE SEVENTH TRUMPET: THE LAST TRUMP

> If anyone worships the beast and its image and receives a mark on his forehead or on his hand, ¹⁰ he also will drink the wine of God's wrath, poured full strength into the cup of his anger, and he will be tormented with fire and sulfur in the presence of the holy angels and in the presence of the Lamb. ¹¹ And the smoke of their torment goes up forever and ever, and they have no rest, day or night, these worshipers of the beast and its image, and whoever receives the mark of its name. (Rev 14:9–11)

At this point in the eschatological events, God will be wrapping up things to finally take over the earth. To buttress the significance of the destruction of Babylon, there is a great rejoicing in heaven:

> After this I heard what seemed to be the loud voice of a great multitude in heaven, crying out,
> "Hallelujah!
> Salvation and glory and power belong to our God,
> ² for his judgments are true and just;
> for he has judged the great prostitute
>   who corrupted the earth with her immorality,
> and has avenged on her the blood of his servants."
> ³ Once more they cried out,
> "Hallelujah!
> The smoke from her goes up forever and ever."
> ⁴ And the twenty-four elders and the four living creatures fell down and worshiped God who was seated on the throne, saying, "Amen. Hallelujah!" ⁵ And from the throne came a voice saying,
> "Praise our God,
>   all you his servants,
> you who fear him,
>   small and great." (Rev 19:1–5)

This declaration in heaven seems to be reechoing Isaiah's prophecy when God judged Edom (covering present-day Saudi Arabia):

> For the LORD has a day of vengeance, a year of recompense for the cause of Zion.
> ⁹ And the streams of Edom shall be turned into pitch, and her soil into sulfur; her land shall become burning pitch.
> ¹⁰ Night and day it shall not be quenched; its smoke shall go up forever.
> From generation to generation it shall lie waste; none shall pass through it forever and ever. (Isa 34:8–10)

This may also be a pointer that Babylon may not be Jerusalem but a city in Edom (Saudi Arabia).

6.5. THE MARRIAGE SUPPER OF THE LAMB

Then I heard what seemed to be the voice of a great multitude, like the roar of many waters and like the sound of mighty peals of thunder, crying out,
"Hallelujah!
For the Lord our God
   the Almighty reigns.
[7] Let us rejoice and exult
   and give him the glory,
for the marriage of the Lamb has come,
   and his Bride has made herself ready;
[8] it was granted her to clothe herself
   with fine linen, bright and pure"—
for the fine linen is the righteous deeds of the saints.
[9] And the angel said to me, "Write this: Blessed are those who are invited to the marriage supper of the Lamb." And he said to me, "These are the true words of God." [10] Then I fell down at his feet to worship him, but he said to me, "You must not do that! I am a fellow servant with you and your brothers who hold to the testimony of Jesus. Worship God." For the testimony of Jesus is the spirit of prophecy. (Rev 19:6–10)

It is vitally important to note that the marriage supper of the Lamb happens in heaven between Jesus Christ and believers who were martyred during the great tribulation ("the saints who washed their clothes"). And this is after the harvest and before the white rider—Jesus Christ—appears on the stage to defeat the dragon and his armies and take over the reign on earth. Hence, the marriage is between the souls of those who have died from great tribulation and Christ, while their bodies have been buried on earth. This part is really important, as it will help in understanding the resurrection of the dead that will happen before the millennial reign of Christ (§6.8).

6.6. THE SECOND COMING OF JESUS CHRIST

Towards the end of age, Jesus Christ will come riding a white horse with heavenly armies, to take over the control of earth. The second coming of Jesus Christ will commence after the following events: 144,000 Jews have been redeemed from the earth, seven bowls of God's judgment have been unleashed, Babylon the great has been destroyed, and the marriage supper of the Lamb and souls of believers has been completed in heaven. At this point in the eschatological events, the antichrist has long been revealed, and the great tribulation has already occurred. This is the reason Paul had the following to say in 2 Thessalonians:

> Now concerning the coming of our Lord Jesus Christ and our being gathered together to him, we ask you, brothers, ² not to be quickly shaken in mind or alarmed, either by a spirit or a spoken word, or a letter seeming to be from us, to the effect that the day of the Lord has come. ³ Let no one deceive you in any way. For that day will not come, unless the rebellion comes first, and the man of lawlessness is revealed, the son of destruction, ⁴ who opposes and exalts himself against every so-called god or object of worship, so that he takes his seat in the temple of God, proclaiming himself to be God. (2 Thess 2:1–4)

6.6.1. The Rider on a White Horse

> Then I saw heaven opened, and behold, a white horse! The one sitting on it is called Faithful and True, and in righteousness he judges and makes war. ¹² His eyes are like a flame of fire, and on his head are many diadems, and he has a name written that no one knows but himself. ¹³ He is clothed in a robe dipped in blood, and the name by which he is called is The Word of God. ¹⁴ And the armies of heaven, arrayed in fine linen, white and pure, were following him on white horses. ¹⁵ From his mouth comes a sharp sword with which to strike down the nations, and he will rule them with a rod of iron. He will tread the winepress of the fury of the wrath of God the Almighty. ¹⁶ On his robe and on his thigh he has a name written, King of kings and Lord of lords. (Rev 19:11–21)

This rider of the white horse is definitely Jesus Christ and different from the rider of the first white horse found earlier when the first seal was opened (§3.4), which marked the beginning of the end-time events. Unlike the first rider of a white horse (that was given only one crown), this rider of a white horse has so many crowns/diadems on his head. Second, this rider is called The Word of God. Third, "on his robe and on his thigh he has a name written, King of kings and Lord of lords."

A key point to note here is that Christ is coming to the earth with armies of heaven, and not with those who had been martyred returning with him. This means he is coming for a battle. That battle is what is commonly known as the battle of Armageddon, which will lead to the defeat of the antichrist and imprisonment of Satan.

6.6.2. The Battle of Armageddon—The Defeat of the Antichrist and His Armies

> Then I saw an angel standing in the sun, and with a loud voice he called to all the birds that fly directly overhead, "Come, gather for the great supper of God, [18] to eat the flesh of kings, the flesh of captains, the flesh of mighty men, the flesh of horses and their riders, and the flesh of all men, both free and slave, both small and great."
>
> [19] And I saw the beast and the kings of the earth with their armies gathered to make war against him who was sitting on the horse and against his army. [20] And the beast was captured, and with it the false prophet who in its presence had done the signs by which he deceived those who had received the mark of the beast and those who worshiped its image. These two were thrown alive into the lake of fire that burns with sulfur. [21] And the rest were slain by the sword that came from the mouth of him who was sitting on the horse, and all the birds were gorged with their flesh. (Rev 19:17–21)

The preparation for the battle of Armageddon in Satan's camp commences during the sixth bowl (see §6.4.6), when the dragon, the antichrist, and the false prophet go out to gather kings of the earth for the battle.

> And I saw, coming out of the mouth of the dragon and out of the mouth of the beast and out of the mouth of the false prophet, three unclean spirits like frogs. [14] For they are demonic spirits, performing signs, who go abroad to the kings of the whole world, to assemble them for battle on the great day of God the Almighty. (Rev 16:13–14)

> And they assembled them at the *place that in Hebrew is called Armageddon*. (Rev 16:16)

This move by the three entities will be geared towards the establishment of the eighth beast (kingdom/final empire of the antichrist), which

THE SEVENTH TRUMPET: THE LAST TRUMP

is essentially an alliance of nations (confederacy or something of that sort) hinted at in Rev 17 as the beast that would soon go into destruction (see §6.4.8):

> As for the beast that was and is not, it is an eighth but it belongs to the seven, and it goes to destruction. ¹² And the ten horns that you saw are ten kings who have not yet received royal power, but they are to receive authority as kings for one hour, together with the beast. ¹³ These are of one mind, and they hand over their power and authority to the beast. ¹⁴ They will make war on the Lamb, and the Lamb will conquer them, for he is Lord of lords and King of kings, and those with him are called and chosen and faithful. (Rev 17:11–14)

Although not many details are given in Revelation as per how the battle is executed, it is clear that it will be a swift and bloody war. Zechariah did provide some details of the devastating impact of this battle:

> Behold, the day of the LORD cometh, and thy spoil shall be divided in the midst of thee.² For I will gather all nations against Jerusalem to battle; and the city shall be taken, and the houses rifled, and the women ravished; and half of the city shall go forth into captivity, and the residue of the people shall not be cut off from the city.³ Then shall the LORD go forth, and fight against those nations, as when he fought in the day of battle. (Zech 14:1–3 AV)

> And this shall be the plague wherewith the Lord will smite all the people that have fought against Jerusalem; Their flesh shall consume away while they stand upon their feet, and their eyes shall consume away in their holes, and their tongue shall consume away in their mouth.
> ¹³ And it shall come to pass in that day, that a great tumult from the LORD shall be among them; and they shall lay hold every one on the hand of his neighbour, and his hand shall rise up against the hand of his neighbour.
> ¹⁴ And Judah also shall fight at Jerusalem; and the wealth of all the heathen round about shall be gathered together, gold, and silver, and apparel, in great abundance.
> ¹⁵ And so shall be the plague of the horse, of the mule, of the camel, and of the ass, and of all the beasts that shall be in these tents, as this plague.
> ¹⁶ And it shall come to pass, that every one that is left of all the nations which came against Jerusalem shall even go up from

year to year to worship the King, the Lord of hosts, and to keep the feast of tabernacles.

¹⁷ And it shall be, that whoso will not come up of all the families of the earth unto Jerusalem to worship the King, the Lord of hosts, even upon them shall be no rain.

¹⁸ And if the family of Egypt go not up, and come not, that have no rain; there shall be the plague, wherewith the Lord will smite the heathen that come not up to keep the feast of tabernacles.

¹⁹ This shall be the punishment of Egypt, and the punishment of all nations that come not up to keep the feast of tabernacles.

²⁰ In that day shall there be upon the bells of the horses, Holiness Unto The Lord; and the pots in the Lord's house shall be like the bowls before the altar.

²¹ Yea, every pot in Jerusalem and in Judah shall be holiness unto the Lord of hosts: and all they that sacrifice shall come and take of them, and seethe therein: and in that day there shall be no more the Canaanite in the house of the Lord of hosts. (Zech 14:12–21 AV)

In the end, Satan and his cohorts will be defeated. The antichrist and the false prophet will be captured alive and thrown into the lake of fire, and world leaders and their armies slaughtered. However, Satan will be sentenced to one thousand years imprisonment in the bottomless pit:

> Then I saw an angel coming down from heaven, holding in his hand the key to the bottomless pit and a great chain. ² And he seized the dragon, that ancient serpent, who is the devil and Satan, and bound him for a thousand years, ³ and threw him into the pit, and shut it and sealed it over him, so that he might not deceive the nations any longer, until the thousand years were ended. After that he must be released for a little while. (Rev 20:1–3)

This appears to be the fulfilment of Isa 14 where the entity rereferred to as "Day Star, son of Dawn" (Lucifer in AV) who sought to make himself like the Most High was brought low, down to Sheol (to the far reaches of the pit):

> When the Lord has given you rest from your pain and turmoil and the hard service with which you were made to serve, ⁴ you will take up this taunt against the king of Babylon:
> "How the oppressor has ceased,
>   the insolent fury ceased!

⁵ The Lord has broken the staff of the wicked,
    the scepter of rulers,
⁶ that struck the peoples in wrath
    with unceasing blows,
that ruled the nations in anger
    with unrelenting persecution.
⁷ The whole earth is at rest and quiet;
    they break forth into singing.
⁸ The cypresses rejoice at you,
    the cedars of Lebanon, saying,
'Since you were laid low,
    no woodcutter comes up against us.'
⁹ Sheol beneath is stirred up
    to meet you when you come;
it rouses the shades to greet you,
    all who were leaders of the earth;
it raises from their thrones
    all who were kings of the nations.
¹⁰ All of them will answer
    and say to you:
'You too have become as weak as we!
    You have become like us!'
¹¹ Your pomp is brought down to Sheol,
    the sound of your harps;
maggots are laid as a bed beneath you,
    and worms are your covers.
¹² *"How you are fallen from heaven,*
    O Day Star, son of Dawn!
How you are cut down to the ground,
    you who laid the nations low!
¹³ You said in your heart,
    'I will ascend to heaven;
above the stars of God
    I will set my throne on high;
I will sit on the mount of assembly
    in the far reaches of the north;
¹⁴ I will ascend above the heights of the clouds;
    I will make myself like the Most High.'
¹⁵ But you are brought down to Sheol,
    to the far reaches of the pit.
¹⁶ Those who see you will stare at you
    and ponder over you:
'Is this the man who made the earth tremble,
    who shook kingdoms,

> ^{17} who made the world like a desert
> and overthrew its cities,
> who did not let his prisoners go home?'
> ^{18} All the kings of the nations lie in glory,
> each in his own tomb;
> ^{19} but you are cast out, away from your grave,
> like a loathed branch,
> clothed with the slain, those pierced by the sword,
> who go down to the stones of the pit,
> like a dead body trampled underfoot.
> ^{20} You will not be joined with them in burial,
> because you have destroyed your land,
> you have slain your people. (Isa 14:4–20)

This prophecy is clearly referring to a time when Satan (king of Babylon) has been defeated, and his ambition to become God cut short.

The battle of Armageddon also appears to be the same battle that Joel prophesied about, which he said will take place at the Valley of Jehoshaphat (Valley of Decision). The following verse tends to link it with certain snippets in Revelation regarding the preparation for this battle:

> Let the nations stir themselves up and come up to the Valley of Jehoshaphat; for there I will sit to judge all the surrounding nations. ^{13} Put in the sickle, for the harvest is ripe. Go in, tread, for the winepress is full.
> The vats overflow, for their evil is great. ^{14} Multitudes, multitudes, in the valley of decision! For the day of the LORD is near in the valley of decision. ^{15} The sun and the moon are darkened, and the stars withdraw their shining. (Joel 3:12–15)

Revelation 16 shows how Satan, the false prophet and antichrist stirred up the nations to assemble for a battle with Jesus Christ and his army:

> For they are demonic spirits, performing signs, who go abroad to the kings of the whole world, *to assemble them for battle on the great day of God the Almighty.* (Rev 16:14)

The battle of Armageddon is the climax of the judgment/wrath God unleashes upon the antichrist, the false prophet, Satan, and their cohorts for maltreating his children. This judgment commences when the seventh seal is opened (§§5.3 and 5.4) and spans through the seven trumpets period and seven bowls of the wrath of God.

Furthermore, Rev 14 symbolizes the harvest of the good and the judgment of the nations where an angel is asked to use his sickle to gather all the evil people and throw them into the great winepress of God's wrath such that blood can flow to 1600 stadia (about 184 miles; a stadion is about 607 feet or 185 meters):

> Then another angel came out of the temple in heaven, and he too had a sharp sickle. [18] And another angel came out from the altar, the angel who has authority over the fire, and he called with a loud voice to the one who had the sharp sickle, "Put in your sickle and gather the clusters from the vine of the earth, for its grapes are ripe." [19] So the angel swung his sickle across the earth and gathered the grape harvest of the earth and threw it into the great winepress of the wrath of God. [20] And the winepress was trodden outside the city, and blood flowed from the winepress, as high as a horse's bridle, for 1,600 stadia. (Rev 17:14–20)

This ties with Joel's prophecy:

> Put in the sickle, for the harvest is ripe. Go in, tread, for the winepress is full. The vats overflow, for their evil is great. (Joel 3:13)

6.7. THE FIRST RESURRECTION—THE RAPTURE!

> Then I saw thrones, and seated on them were those to whom the authority to judge was committed. Also I saw the souls of those who had been beheaded for the testimony of Jesus and for the word of God, and those who had not worshiped the beast or its image and had not received its mark on their foreheads or their hands. They came to life and reigned with Christ for a thousand years. [5] The rest of the dead did not come to life until the thousand years were ended. This is the first resurrection. [6] Blessed and holy is the one who shares in the first resurrection! Over such the second death has no power, but they will be priests of God and of Christ, and they will reign with him for a thousand years. (Rev 20:4–6)

After the battle of Armageddon and the imprisonment of Satan for a thousand years in the bottomless pit, believers, including those who died (beheaded) during the great tribulation for their faith in Christ will be resurrected ("come to life") and joined with those alive, who did "not worship the beast or its image and had not received its mark on their foreheads or their hands." Both the living and the resurrected will be transformed into a different kind of humans (with an imperishable and immortal body). This body is similar to the body Christ had after his resurrection and possibly the type of body Adam initially had before he was cast out of garden of Eden. What happens during this event was elaborated on by St. Paul:

> ⁵I tell you this, brothers: flesh and blood cannot inherit the kingdom of God, nor does the perishable inherit the imperishable. ⁵¹ Behold! I tell you a mystery. We shall not all sleep, but we shall all be changed, ⁵² in a moment, in the twinkling of an eye, at the last trumpet. For the trumpet will sound, and the dead will be raised imperishable, and we shall be changed. ⁵³ For this perishable body must put on the imperishable, and this mortal body must put on immortality. (1 Cor 15:50–54)

If rapture means the event that will orchestrate the transformation of humans to a higher spiritual level, this event is actually the so-called rapture. During this event, both the dead and the living shall be transformed into an elevated version of humans (with resurrected bodies). This body will most likely be the same body that Jesus Christ had after his resurrection:

> For this we declare to you by a word from the Lord, that we who are alive, who are left until the coming of the Lord, will not precede those who have fallen asleep. ¹⁶For the Lord himself will descend from heaven with a cry of command, with the voice of an archangel, and with the sound of the trumpet of God. And the dead in Christ will rise first. Then we who are alive, who are left, will be caught up together with them in the clouds to meet the Lord in the air. (1 Thess 4:15–16)

Hence, this first resurrection is the point where believers are restored to the original state of humanity that Adam had at creation, before the fall (the fall brought man to a lower state, below what he was originally created to operate in). Hence, the whole purpose of the great tribulation may be to sieve through humans to select those that will be restored to man's original state. Peter aptly captured this:

> Blessed be the God and Father of our Lord Jesus Christ! According to his great mercy, he has caused us to be born again to a living hope through the resurrection of Jesus Christ from the dead, ⁴ *to an inheritance that is imperishable, undefiled, and unfading, kept in heaven for you,* ⁵ who by God's power are being guarded through faith for *a salvation ready to be revealed in the last time.* ⁶ In this you rejoice, though now for a little while, if necessary, you *have been grieved by various trials,* ⁷ *so that the tested genuineness of your faith—more precious than gold that perishes though it is tested by fire—may be found to result in praise*

THE SEVENTH TRUMPET: THE LAST TRUMP 149

and glory and honor at the revelation of Jesus Christ. ⁸ *Though you have not seen him, you love him. Though you do not now see him, you believe in him and rejoice with joy that is inexpressible and filled with glory,* ⁹ *obtaining the outcome of your faith, the salvation of your souls.* (1 Pet 1:3–9).

The book of Sirach also noted:

When a sieve is shaken, the husks appear;
 so do one's faults when one speaks.
As the test of what the potter moulds is in the furnace,
 so in tribulation is the test of the just. (Sirach 27:4–5 CPVD)

A second resurrection is also hinted at here, where those who followed the antichrist and Satan will be raised to face the final judgment:

The rest of the dead did not come to life until the thousand years were ended. This is the first resurrection. ⁶ Blessed and holy is the one who shares in the first resurrection! Over such the second death has no power, but they will be priests of God and of Christ, and they will reign with him for a thousand years. (Rev 20:4–6)

And many of those who sleep in the dust of the earth shall awake, some to everlasting life, and some to shame and everlasting contempt. (Dan 12:2)

6.8. THE MILLENNIAL REIGN

The millennial reign is a period of one thousand years after the battle of Armageddon when Christ will rule the earth alongside his followers:

Then I saw thrones, and seated on them were those to whom the authority to judge was committed. *Also I saw the souls of those who had been beheaded for the testimony of Jesus and for the word of God, and those who had not worshiped the beast or its image and had not received its mark on their foreheads or their hands. They came to life and reigned with Christ for a thousand years.* ⁵ The rest of the dead did not come to life until the thousand years were ended. This is the first resurrection. (Rev 20:4–6)

Not much detail of this reign is given in Revelation; however, Ezek 40–48 seems to provide elaborate details of the state of affairs in Israel (including the design for the temple and division of the land in Israel) when the millennial reign kicks off. This period will be a period of peace and harmony across the world, as Satan and his cohorts will have been removed from the earth and God fully taken control. This period will probably be similar to the period when Adam and Eve were in the garden of Eden.

This period was prophesied by many prophets in the Bible such as Zechariah, Isaiah, and Daniel. Zechariah prophesied that Jesus would return to the earth and set his feet on the Mount of Olives before Jerusalem (Zech 14:4) and that he would return to earth to be King and one Lord over all the earth (Zech 14:9):

> Behold, the day of the Lord cometh, and thy spoil shall be divided in the midst of thee. ² For I will gather all nations against Jerusalem to battle; and the city shall be taken, and the houses rifled, and the women ravished; and half of the city shall go forth into captivity, and the residue of the people shall not be cut off from the city. ³ Then shall the Lord go forth, and fight against those nations, as when he fought in the day of battle. ⁴ And his feet shall stand in that day upon the mount of Olives, which is before Jerusalem on the east, and the mount of Olives shall cleave in the midst thereof toward the east and toward the west, and there shall be a very great valley; and half of the mountain shall remove toward the north, and half of it toward the south. ⁵ And ye shall flee to the valley of the mountains; for the valley of the mountains shall reach unto Azal: yea, ye shall flee, like as ye fled from before the earthquake in the days of Uzziah king of Judah: and the Lord my God shall come, and all the saints with thee. (Zech 14:1–5 AV)

> *And the Lord will be king over all the earth.* On that day the Lord will be one and his name one. (Zech 14:9)

Isaiah prophesied thus:

> For to us a child is born, to us a son is given; and the government shall be upon his shoulder, and his name shall be called Wonderful Counselor, Mighty God, Everlasting Father, Prince of Peace.
> ⁷ Of the increase of his government and of peace there will be no end, on the throne of David and over his kingdom, to establish it and to uphold it with justice and with righteousness from this time forth and forevermore.
> The zeal of the Lord of hosts will do this. (Isa 9:6–7)

Daniel also prophesied about this kingdom, which was established after the antichrist has been defeated:

> I looked then because of the sound of the great words that the horn was speaking. And as I looked, the beast was killed, and its body destroyed and given over to be burned with fire. [12] As for the rest of the beasts, their dominion was taken away, but their lives were prolonged for a season and a time.
> [13] I saw in the night visions, and behold, with the clouds of heaven there came one like a son of man, and he came to the Ancient of Days and was presented before him.
> [14] And to him was given dominion and glory and a kingdom, that all peoples, nations, and languages should serve him; his dominion is an everlasting dominion, which shall not pass away, and his kingdom one that shall not be destroyed. (Dan 7:11–14)

6.9. THE RETURN OF SATAN AND THE FINAL ANGELIC WAR ON EARTH—THE GOG AND MAGOG WAR

> And when the thousand years are ended, Satan will be released from his prison [8] and will come out to deceive the nations that are at the four corners of the earth, Gog and Magog, to gather them for battle; their number is like the sand of the sea. [9] And they marched up over the broad plain of the earth and surrounded the camp of the saints and the beloved city, but fire came down from heaven and consumed them, [10] and the devil who had deceived them was thrown into the lake of fire and sulfur where the beast and the false prophet were, and they will be tormented day and night forever and ever. (Rev 20:7–10)

At the expiration of the thousand-year imprisonment, Satan will be released from the bottomless pit. He will return on earth to deceive the nations once again. This will eventually lead to the final war on earth, the so-called Gog and Magog War prophesied by Ezekiel:

> And the word of the LORD came unto me, saying,[2] Son of man, set thy face against Gog, the land of Magog, the chief prince of Meshech and Tubal, and prophesy against him,[3] And say, Thus saith the Lord GOD; Behold, I am against thee, O Gog, the chief prince of Meshech and Tubal: [4] And I will turn thee back, and put hooks into thy jaws, and I will bring thee forth, and all thine

army, horses and horsemen, all of them clothed with all sorts of armour, even a great company with bucklers and shields, all of them handling swords:[5] Persia, Ethiopia, and Libya with them; all of them with shield and helmet:[6] Gomer, and all his bands; the house of Togarmah of the north quarters, and all his bands: and many people with thee.

[7] Be thou prepared, and prepare for thyself, thou, and all thy company that are assembled unto thee, and be thou a guard unto them.[8] After many days thou shalt be visited: in the latter years thou shalt come into the land that is brought back from the sword, and is gathered out of many people, against the mountains of Israel, which have been always waste: but it is brought forth out of the nations, and they shall dwell safely all of them.[9] Thou shalt ascend and come like a storm, thou shalt be like a cloud to cover the land, thou, and all thy bands, and many people with thee.

[10] Thus saith the Lord God; It shall also come to pass, that at the same time shall things come into thy mind, and thou shalt think an evil thought: [11] And thou shalt say, I will go up to the land of unwalled villages; I will go to them that are at rest, that dwell safely, all of them dwelling without walls, and having neither bars nor gates,[12] To take a spoil, and to take a prey; to turn thine hand upon the desolate places that are now inhabited, and upon the people that are gathered out of the nations, which have gotten cattle and goods, that dwell in the midst of the land.[13] Sheba, and Dedan, and the merchants of Tarshish, with all the young lions thereof, shall say unto thee, Art thou come to take a spoil? hast thou gathered thy company to take a prey? to carry away silver and gold, to take away cattle and goods, to take a great spoil?

[14] Therefore, son of man, prophesy and say unto Gog, Thus saith the Lord God; In that day when my people of Israel dwelleth safely, shalt thou not know it?[15] And thou shalt come from thy place out of the north parts, thou, and many people with thee, all of them riding upon horses, a great company, and a mighty army:[16] And thou shalt come up against my people of Israel, as a cloud to cover the land; it shall be in the latter days, and I will bring thee against my land, that the heathen may know me, when I shall be sanctified in thee, O Gog, before their eyes.

[17] Thus saith the Lord God; Art thou he of whom I have spoken in old time by my servants the prophets of Israel, which prophesied in those days many years that I would bring thee against them? [18] And it shall come to pass at the same time when Gog shall come against the land of Israel, saith the Lord God,

> that my fury shall come up in my face.[19] For in my jealousy and in the fire of my wrath have I spoken, Surely in that day there shall be a great shaking in the land of Israel; [20] So that the fishes of the sea, and the fowls of the heaven, and the beasts of the field, and all creeping things that creep upon the earth, and all the men that are upon the face of the earth, shall shake at my presence, and the mountains shall be thrown down, and the steep places shall fall, and every wall shall fall to the ground. [21] And I will call for a sword against him throughout all my mountains, saith the Lord God: every man's sword shall be against his brother.[22] And I will plead against him with pestilence and with blood; and I will rain upon him, and upon his bands, and upon the many people that are with him, an overflowing rain, and great hailstones, fire, and brimstone. [23] Thus will I magnify myself, and sanctify myself; and I will be known in the eyes of many nations, and they shall know that I am the Lord. (Ezek 38:1-23 AV)

This verse seems to suggest that the followers of Christ at this time will all be in Israel, and unbelievers will be residing outside this place.

That there will be unbelieving nations after the battle of Armageddon can be gleaned from Zechariah:

> And it shall come to pass, that every one that is left of all the nations which came against Jerusalem shall even go up from year to year to worship the King, the Lord of hosts, and to keep the feast of tabernacles. [17] And it shall be, that whoso will not come up of all the families of the earth unto Jerusalem to worship the King, the Lord of hosts, even upon them shall be no rain. [18] And if the family of Egypt go not up, and come not, that have no rain; there shall be the plague, wherewith the Lord will smite the heathen that come not up to keep the feast of tabernacles.[19] This shall be the punishment of Egypt, and the punishment of all nations that come not up to keep the feast of tabernacles. (Zech 14:16-19 AV)

Hence, when Satan is released from the bottomless pit, he will be able to muster forces from the unbelieving nations to attack Jerusalem. However, he will be ultimately defeated and finally thrown into the lake of fire. His followers will also be judged and thrown into the lake of fire.

6.10. THE SECOND RESURRECTION AND FINAL JUDGMENT

> Then I saw a great white throne and him who was seated on it. From his presence earth and sky fled away, and no place was found for them. ^{12} And I saw the dead, great and small, standing before the throne, and books were opened. Then another book was opened, which is the book of life. And the dead were judged by what was written in the books, according to what they had done. ^{13} And the sea gave up the dead who were in it, Death and Hades gave up the dead who were in them, and they were judged, each one of them, according to what they had done. ^{14} Then Death and Hades were thrown into the lake of fire. This is the second death, the lake of fire. ^{15} And if anyone's name was not found written in the book of life, he was thrown into the lake of fire. (Rev 20:11–15)

This event is popularly referred to as the white throne judgment. This is the event where every person that has lived on earth will be judged for their deeds. The dead who were not resurrected during the first resurrection (see §6.7) will be raised to face their judgment. Anyone whose deeds did not meet up to the standard of God (their names not found in the book of life) will be thrown into the lake of fire, where the antichrist, false prophet, Satan, Hades, and death have all been thrown in. This event was hinted at by Jesus Christ using the parable of the talents, and that of the sheep and goats:

> *When the Son of Man comes in his glory, and all the angels with him, then he will sit on his glorious throne. ^{32} Before him will be gathered all the nations, and he will separate people one from another as a shepherd separates the sheep from the goats. ^{33} And he will place the sheep on his right, but the goats on the left. ^{34} Then the King will say to those on his right, "Come, you who are blessed by my Father, inherit the kingdom prepared for you from the foundation of the world." (Matt 25:31–34)*

> Then he will say to those on his left, "Depart from me, you cursed, into the eternal fire prepared for the devil and his angels." (Matt 25:41)

6.11. THE NEW EARTH AND NEW HEAVEN

Then I saw a new heaven and a new earth, for the first heaven and the first earth had passed away, and the sea was no more. ² And I saw the holy city, new Jerusalem, coming down out of heaven from God, prepared as a bride adorned for her husband. ³ And I heard a loud voice from the throne saying, "Behold, the dwelling place of God is with man. He will dwell with them, and they will be his people, and God himself will be with them as their God. ⁴ He will wipe away every tear from their eyes, and death shall be no more, neither shall there be mourning, nor crying, nor pain anymore, for the former things have passed away."

⁵ And he who was seated on the throne said, "Behold, I am making all things new." Also he said, "Write this down, for these words are trustworthy and true." ⁶ And he said to me, "It is done! I am the Alpha and the Omega, the beginning and the end. To the thirsty I will give from the spring of the water of life without payment. ⁷ The one who conquers will have this heritage, and I will be his God and he will be my son. ⁸ But as for the cowardly, the faithless, the detestable, as for murderers, the sexually immoral, sorcerers, idolaters, and all liars, their portion will be in the lake that burns with fire and sulfur, which is the second death." (Rev 21:1–8)

The present earth having come to its end at the completion of the millennial era will give way to a new earth and a new heaven created by God. Hence, a new age devoid of Satan and evil will commence. This is like the beginning of another cycle. God will dwell with man in this new earth "and death shall be no more, neither shall there be mourning, nor crying, nor pain anymore, for the former things have passed away."

7

Exegesis

7.1. THE RETURN OF EDEN—NEW JERUSALEM

Then came one of the seven angels who had the seven bowls full of the seven last plagues and spoke to me, saying, "Come, I will show you the Bride, the wife of the Lamb." [10] And he carried me away in the Spirit to a great, high mountain, and showed me the holy city Jerusalem coming down out of heaven from God, [11] having the glory of God, its radiance like a most rare jewel, like a jasper, clear as crystal. [12] It had a great, high wall, with twelve gates, and at the gates twelve angels, and on the gates the names of the twelve tribes of the sons of Israel were inscribed— [13] on the east three gates, on the north three gates, on the south three gates, and on the west three gates. [14] And the wall of the city had twelve foundations, and on them were the twelve names of the twelve apostles of the Lamb.

[15] And the one who spoke with me had a measuring rod of gold to measure the city and its gates and walls. [16] The city lies foursquare, its length the same as its width. And he measured the city with his rod, 12,000 stadia. Its length and width and height are equal. [17] He also measured its wall, 144 cubits by human measurement, which is also an angel's measurement. [18] The wall was built of jasper, while the city was pure gold, like clear glass. [19] The foundations of the wall of the city were adorned with every kind of jewel. The first was jasper, the second sapphire, the third agate, the fourth emerald, [20] the fifth onyx, the

sixth carnelian, the seventh chrysolite, the eighth beryl, the ninth topaz, the tenth chrysoprase, the eleventh jacinth, the twelfth amethyst. ²¹ And the twelve gates were twelve pearls, each of the gates made of a single pearl, and the street of the city was pure gold, like transparent glass.

²² And I saw no temple in the city, for its temple is the Lord God the Almighty and the Lamb. ²³ And the city has no need of sun or moon to shine on it, for the glory of God gives it light, and its lamp is the Lamb. ²⁴ By its light will the nations walk, and the kings of the earth will bring their glory into it, ²⁵ and its gates will never be shut by day—and there will be no night there. ²⁶ They will bring into it the glory and the honor of the nations. ²⁷ But nothing unclean will ever enter it, nor anyone who does what is detestable or false, but only those who are written in the Lamb's book of life. (Rev 21:9-27)

7.2. THE RIVER OF LIFE

Then the angel showed me the river of the water of life, bright as crystal, flowing from the throne of God and of the Lamb ² through the middle of the street of the city; also, on either side of the river, the tree of life with its twelve kinds of fruit, yielding its fruit each month. The leaves of the tree were for the healing of the nations. ³ No longer will there be anything accursed, but the throne of God and of the Lamb will be in it, and his servants will worship him. ⁴ They will see his face, and his name will be on their foreheads. ⁵ And night will be no more. They will need no light of lamp or sun, for the Lord God will be their light, and they will reign forever and ever. (Rev 22:1-5)

7.3. THESE WORDS ARE TRUSTWORTHY— JESUS IS COMING

And he said to me, "These words are trustworthy and true. And the Lord, the God of the spirits of the prophets, has sent his angel to show his servants what must soon take place."

⁷ "And behold, I am coming soon. Blessed is the one who keeps the words of the prophecy of this book."

⁸ I, John, am the one who heard and saw these things. And when I heard and saw them, I fell down to worship at the feet of the angel who showed them to me, ⁹ but he said to me, "You must not do that! I am a fellow servant with you and your brothers the prophets, and with those who keep the words of this book. Worship God."

¹⁰ And he said to me, "Do not seal up the words of the prophecy of this book, for the time is near. ¹¹ Let the evildoer still do evil, and the filthy still be filthy, and the righteous still do right, and the holy still be holy."

¹² "Behold, I am coming soon, bringing my recompense with me, to repay each one for what he has done. ¹³ I am the Alpha and the Omega, the first and the last, the beginning and the end."

¹⁴ Blessed are those who wash their robes, so that they may have the right to the tree of life and that they may enter the city by the gates. ¹⁵ Outside are the dogs and sorcerers and the sexually immoral and murderers and idolaters, and everyone who loves and practices falsehood.

¹⁶ "I, Jesus, have sent my angel to testify to you about these things for the churches. I am the root and the descendant of David, the bright morning star."

¹⁷ The Spirit and the Bride say, "Come." And let the one who hears say, "Come." And let the one who is thirsty come; let the one who desires take the water of life without price.

¹⁸ I warn everyone who hears the words of the prophecy of this book: if anyone adds to them, God will add to him the plagues described in this book, ¹⁹ and if anyone takes away from the words of the book of this prophecy, God will take away his share in the tree of life and in the holy city, which are described in this book.

²⁰ He who testifies to these things says, "Surely I am coming soon." Amen. Come, Lord Jesus!

²¹ The grace of the Lord Jesus be with all. Amen. (Rev 22:1–21)

7.4. GOD EXPECTS PEOPLE TO REPENT DURING THE EVENT OF THE END-TIME

All through the wrath period, it seems that God is on the lookout for people who will repent. At the end of the events of the sixth trumpet, John notes thus:

> The rest of mankind, who were not killed by these plagues, did not repent of the works of their hands nor give up worshiping demons and idols of gold and silver and bronze and stone and wood, which cannot see or hear or walk, [21] nor did they repent of their murders or their sorceries or their sexual immorality or their thefts. (Rev 9:20–21)

This means that there is an expectation from God that having passed through perilous moments, some people will seek the face of God and repent. However, this is not the case. Hence, it is safe to assume that anyone who does not take the mark of the beast and accepts Christ will be saved, even at this time.

7.5. MEETING JESUS IN THE CLOUDS IS NOT RAPTURE

The cliché of "meeting the Lord in the clouds/air," which has permeated Christian beliefs and doctrines, has brought a lot of confusion to Christians. The cliché stems mainly from the misunderstanding of the following passage from Paul's Epistle to Thessalonians:

> For since we believe that Jesus died and rose again, even so, through Jesus, God will bring with him those who have fallen asleep. [15] For this we declare to you by a word from the Lord, that we who are alive, who are left until the coming of the Lord, will not precede those who have fallen asleep.
> [16] For the Lord himself will descend from heaven with a cry of command, with the voice of an archangel, and with the sound of the trumpet of God. And the dead in Christ will rise first. [17] Then we who are alive, who are left, will be caught up together with them in the clouds to meet the Lord in the air, and so we will always be with the Lord. [18] Therefore encourage one another with these words. (1 Thess 4:14–18)

This is one of the key bases for the rapture theory. However, interpretation of this passage as a justification for rapture is faulty and conflicts with various eschatological accounts presented in the Bible, including direct quotes of Jesus Christ and the presentations in the book of Revelation. A careful reading of this passage will show that this verse is actually referring to the first resurrection (see §6.7), which happens after the great tribulation and battle of Armageddon.

Simply put, this is one of the last events before the establishment of the millennial reign of Christ. Key points that jump out of this event as reported by Paul are:

- Resurrection of the dead in Christ
- The resurrected and those still alive will meet the Lord in air/clouds
- These people will remain with Christ from that point always.

These align with what John reports in the book of Revelation:

> Then I saw thrones, and seated on them were those to whom the authority to judge was committed. Also I saw *the souls of those who had been beheaded for the testimony of Jesus and for the word of God, and those who had not worshiped the beast or its image and had not received its mark on their foreheads or their hands. They came to life and reigned with Christ for a thousand years.* [5] The rest of the dead did not come to life until the thousand years were ended. This is the first resurrection. (Rev 20:4–5)

Hence, these two events are the same. Taking this further, the idea of meeting the Lord in air or clouds as presented by Paul does not necessarily translate to meeting the Lord in heaven, because Christ will have already left heaven to take up his throne on earth:

> For the Lord himself will descend from heaven with a cry of command, with the voice of an archangel, and with the sound of the trumpet of God. (1 Thess 4:16)

It may be that during and after the battle of Armageddon, Christ may be hovering in the air watching as his army battles Satan's army. Recall that at the last mention of Christ in the revelation, before the first resurrection, he is presented as riding out of heaven:

> Then I saw heaven opened, and behold, a white horse! The one sitting on it is called Faithful and True, and in righteousness he judges and makes war. [12] His eyes are like a flame of fire, and on his head are many diadems, and he has a name written that no one knows but himself. (Rev 19:11–12)

Thus, if Paul says the dead and the living will be caught up with Christ in the air, that should not be a source of confusion. Christ's foot eventually touches the ground to set up his kingdom, according to Zechariah:

> Then shall the LORD go forth, and fight against those nations, as when he fought in the day of battle. [4] And his feet shall stand in that day upon the mount of Olives, which is before Jerusalem on the east, and the mount of Olives shall cleave in the midst thereof toward the east and toward the west, and there shall be a

very great valley; and half of the mountain shall remove toward the north, and half of it toward the south. (Zech 14:3–4 AV)

Also note that Christ sets his foot on a mountain, which is above ground. Hence, meeting the Lord in the air/clouds might be referring to believers joining up with Christ on the mountain. The rapture theory has run into a lot of controversy as people try to reinterpret and understand it. This has led to multiple versions of the rapture theory. In trying to reconcile this belief that the "meeting the Lord in the air" justifies the rapture, with other eschatology events, many have been led to believe that Christ will come twice: firstly, to take Christians to heaven before the great tribulation during the so-called rapture, and second to return after the great tribulation to establish his millennial reign. However, as we have seen from the foregoing, it is difficult to find a biblical basis/justification for this type of rapture, whether in the Gospels, epistles, Revelation, or from the books of the prophets that touch on eschatological events. Christ had the following to tell his disciples:

> And there will be signs in sun and moon and stars, and on the earth distress of nations in perplexity because of the roaring of the sea and the waves, [26] people fainting with fear and with foreboding of what is coming on the world. For the powers of the heavens will be shaken. [27] And then they will see the Son of Man coming in a cloud with power and great glory. [28] Now when these things begin to take place, straighten up and raise your heads, because your redemption is drawing near. (Luke 21:25–28).

Conventional rapture theories tend to imply that either before the great tribulation or midpoint during the tribulation or after the great Tribulation, Christ will leave the heavenly abode and Christians will be taken up to meet him in the clouds and possibly taken to heaven. However, in all Christ's teaching about end-time events, there is no indication of this. Rather, this meeting of Christians and Christ will happen only towards the end of the events within the earthly space, as Christ *must* leave heaven for this to happen.

Christ was amply clear about when the gathering of Christians will happen ("after that tribulation"):

> But in those days, *after that tribulation*, the sun will be darkened, and the moon will not give its light, [25] and the stars will be falling from heaven, and the powers in the heavens will be shaken. [26] *And then they will see the Son of Man coming in clouds with*

> *great power and glory.* ²⁷ And then he will send out the angels and gather his elect from the four winds, from the ends of the earth to the ends of heaven. (Mark 13:24–27)

It is also clear from the following verses that Christ was referring to those Christians who were not killed during the persecution of the great tribulation, and not those raptured to heaven:

> ²⁹ So also, when you see these things taking place, you know that he is near, at the very gates. (Mark 13:29)

> For the powers of the heavens will be shaken. ²⁷And then *they will see the Son of Man coming in a cloud with power and great glory.* ²⁸Now when these things begin to take place, straighten up and raise your heads, because your redemption is drawing near." (Luke 21:26–28)

As if to hammer this in, Paul used chapter 15 of his First Letter to the Corinthians to elaborate extensively on the resurrection of the followers of Christ towards the end:

> But in fact Christ has been raised from the dead, the firstfruits of those who have fallen asleep. ²¹ For as by a man came death, by a man has come also the resurrection of the dead. ²² For as in Adam all die, so also in Christ shall all be made alive. ²³ But each in his own order: Christ the firstfruits, then at his coming those who belong to Christ. ²⁴ Then comes the end, when he delivers the kingdom to God the Father after destroying every rule and every authority and power. ²⁵ For he must reign until he has put all his enemies under his feet. ²⁶ The last enemy to be destroyed is death. ²⁷ For "God has put all things in subjection under his feet." But when it says, "all things are put in subjection," it is plain that he is excepted who put all things in subjection under him. ²⁸ When all things are subjected to him, then the Son himself will also be subjected to him who put all things in subjection under him, that God may be all in all. (1 Cor 15:20–28)

The core of his discourse was that at the end, both the living and the dead will be transformed from the earthly body to a heavenly/spiritual body that is imperishable. There was no place within this discussion or elsewhere in his letter that Paul argued for a rapture that would serve as an escape route for Christians. As a matter of fact, the event being discussed in 1 Cor 15:50–55 tallies with the event that Paul hinted at in 1 Thess 4:14–18:

I tell you this, brothers: flesh and blood cannot inherit the kingdom of God, nor does the perishable inherit the imperishable. [51] Behold! I tell you a mystery. *We shall not all sleep, but we shall all be changed,* [52] *in a moment, in the twinkling of an eye, at the last trumpet. For the trumpet will sound, and the dead will be raised imperishable, and we shall be changed.* [53] For this perishable body must put on the imperishable, and this mortal body must put on immortality. [54] When the perishable puts on the imperishable, and the mortal puts on immortality, then shall come to pass the saying that is written:
"Death is swallowed up in victory."
[55] "O death, where is your victory?
O death, where is your sting?" (1 Cor 15:50–55)

There is really no rapture to heaven to escape the great tribulation as many have been led to believe. Christ expects Christians to endure the persecutions. The meeting of Christ in the clouds will happen at a point when Christ has left heaven to establish his kingdom on earth. This event follows the battle of Armageddon where Satan and his armies are defeated, and the antichrist and false prophet cast into the lake of fire. This event is part of the seventh seal event—the time of wrath and judgment.

Christ will not leave heaven until the marriage supper with souls of those who were slain in the great tribulation has been concluded (§6.5). This event is contained within the seventh trumpet events.

The crucial evidence to this is often missed—the seventh seal! The seventh seal is the last seal of the scroll that contains the blueprint for end-time events. And only Jesus can open the seal. Revelation 8 starts by saying the Lamb opens the seventh seal:

> When the Lamb opened the seventh seal, there was silence in heaven for about half an hour. [2] Then I saw the seven angels who stand before God, and seven trumpets were given to them. (Rev 8:1–2)

Thus, if Jesus were still in heaven when the seventh seal is opened, the rapture can't have taken place before then. The time Jesus Christ finally leaves the throne is further down the line in the events of the end-time:

> Then I looked, and behold, a white cloud, and seated on the cloud one like a son of man, with a golden crown on his head, and a sharp sickle in his hand. (Rev 14:14)

The whole purpose of the end-time teachings from Christ is to prepare Christians to face the great tribulation. If he had a rapture prepared for

Christians to escape the great tribulation, he would not have bothered to lay out the details of the sequence of events while alive, as well as revealing it in greater detail to John in Revelation.

7.6. PERSECUTION WILL COME

Behold, I am sending you out as sheep in the midst of wolves, so be wise as serpents and innocent as doves. [17] Beware of men, for they will deliver you over to courts and flog you in their synagogues, [18] and you will be dragged before governors and kings for my sake, to bear witness before them and the Gentiles. [19] When they deliver you over, do not be anxious how you are to speak or what you are to say, for what you are to say will be given to you in that hour. [20] For it is not you who speak, but the Spirit of your Father speaking through you. [21] Brother will deliver brother over to death, and the father his child, and children will rise against parents and have them put to death, [22] and you will be hated by all for my name's sake. But the one who endures to the end will be saved. [23] When they persecute you in one town, flee to the next, for truly, I say to you, you will not have gone through all the towns of Israel before the Son of Man comes.

[24] A disciple is not above his teacher, nor a servant above his master. [25] It is enough for the disciple to be like his teacher, and the servant like his master. If they have called the master of the house Beelzebul, how much more will they malign those of his household.

[26] So have no fear of them, for nothing is covered that will not be revealed, or hidden that will not be known. [27] What I tell you in the dark, say in the light, and what you hear whispered, proclaim on the housetops. [28] And do not fear those who kill the body but cannot kill the soul. Rather fear him who can destroy both soul and body in hell. [29] Are not two sparrows sold for a penny? And not one of them will fall to the ground apart from your Father. [30] But even the hairs of your head are all numbered. [31] Fear not, therefore; you are of more value than many sparrows. [32] So everyone who acknowledges me before men, I also will acknowledge before my Father who is in heaven, [33] but whoever denies me before men, I also will deny before my Father who is in heaven. (Matt 10:16–26)

7.7. VALLEY OF DECISION JOSEPHAT

"For behold, in those days and at that time,
When I bring back the captives of Judah and Jerusalem,
² I will also gather all nations,
And bring them down to the Valley of Jehoshaphat;
And I will enter into judgment with them there
On account of My people, My heritage Israel,
Whom they have scattered among the nations;
They have also divided up My land.
³ They have cast lots for My people,
Have given a boy as payment for a harlot,
And sold a girl for wine, that they may drink.
⁴ Indeed, what have you to do with Me,
O Tyre and Sidon, and all the coasts of Philistia?
Will you retaliate against Me?
But if you retaliate against Me,
Swiftly and speedily I will return your retaliation upon your own head;
⁵ Because you have taken My silver and My gold,
And have carried into your temples My prized possessions.
⁶ Also the people of Judah and the people of Jerusalem
You have sold to the Greeks,
That you may remove them far from their borders.
⁷ Behold, I will raise them
Out of the place to which you have sold them,
And will return your retaliation upon your own head.
⁸ I will sell your sons and your daughters
Into the hand of the people of Judah,
And they will sell them to the Sabeans,
To a people far off;
For the LORD has spoken."
⁹ Proclaim this among the nations:
"Prepare for war!
Wake up the mighty men,
Let all the men of war draw near,
Let them come up.
¹⁰ Beat your plowshares into swords
And your pruning hooks into spears;
Let the weak say, 'I am strong.'"
¹¹ Assemble and come, all you nations,
And gather together all around.
Cause Your mighty ones to go down there, O LORD.

¹² "Let the nations be wakened, and come up to the Valley of Jehoshaphat;
For there I will sit to judge all the surrounding nations.
¹³ Put in the sickle, for the harvest is ripe.
Come, go down;
For the winepress is full,
The vats overflow—
For their wickedness is great."
¹⁴ Multitudes, multitudes in the valley of decision!
For the day of the Lord is near in the valley of decision.
¹⁵ The sun and moon will grow dark,
And the stars will diminish their brightness.
¹⁶ The Lord also will roar from Zion,
And utter His voice from Jerusalem;
The heavens and earth will shake;
But the Lord will be a shelter for His people,
And the strength of the children of Israel.
¹⁷ "So you shall know that I am the Lord your God,
Dwelling in Zion My holy mountain.
Then Jerusalem shall be holy,
And no aliens shall ever pass through her again."
¹⁸ And it will come to pass in that day
That the mountains shall drip with new wine,
The hills shall flow with milk,
And all the brooks of Judah shall be flooded with water;
A fountain shall flow from the house of the Lord
And water the Valley of Acacias.
¹⁹ "Egypt shall be a desolation,
And Edom a desolate wilderness,
Because of violence against the people of Judah,
For they have shed innocent blood in their land.
²⁰ But Judah shall abide forever,
And Jerusalem from generation to generation.
²¹ For I will acquit them of the guilt of bloodshed, whom I had not acquitted;
For the Lord dwells in Zion." (Joel 3:1–21 NKJV)

7.8. WHAT IS THE ROLE OF RUSSIA, UNITED STATES, CHINA, AND EUROPE IN END-TIME EVENTS?

There seems to be an expectation among biblical scholars that current superpowers in the world will play prominent roles in events of the end-time.

However, there is confusion on where to place these superpowers (e.g., Russia, United States, China, and the European Union) in the end-time events, as none of them was directly mentioned when the prophecies of the end-time were reeled out. Geographically and politically, these countries were not even existing as they are today. The biblical end-time prophecies are essentially Near East-centric, either because that was the limit of scope of the prophets receiving these messages or God did not factor these current superpowers into the equation.

If God did not factor these current influential countries into the equation, what would be the import of this? One conclusion that could be extracted from this is that the current great powers of these countries will greatly be whittled down before the key events of the end-time commence, and power will have shifted to countries in the Near East. Another conclusion, which is more likely, is that these world powers will ally with the key players in the Near East, who will prominently feature in the end-time conflict. Hence, directly mentioning them in the prophecies would have been inconsequential, considering that most of them were inconspicuous at the time of the prophecies. There are three key countries in the Near East that are prominent players in end-time: Iran (Persia), Turkey (representing Javan—see §3.5.1), and Israel. It is easy to see how the superpowers can ally with any of these countries. NATO countries could ally with Turkey or Israel if any conflict arises between these two countries and others. Russia and China could ally with Iran. There is already a tripartite pact between Iran, Russia, and China. As a matter of fact, Navies from Iran's armed forces and Revolutionary Guards took part in the 2022 Marine Security Belt exercise with Russian and Chinese Navies that commenced in January 2022.[1]

The current conflict between Russia and Ukraine has exposed fault lines and possible future alliances across the world, with NATO countries going against Russia, while China, India, and Iran are tacitly supporting Russia.

Many biblical scholars have tried to force some countries into the prophecies, even though such countries were not mentioned in the prophecies. A prominent case is the attempt to insert Russia as the key country that will attack Israel or usher in the antichrist. Some have gone as far as referring to Russia's current leader Vladmir Putin as Gog who will lead other countries in a crucial war against Israel.

This is based on the following prophecy from Ezekiel:

> The word of the LORD came to me: ² "Son of man, set your face toward Gog, of the land of Magog, the chief prince

---

1. Hamed, "How Will Russia."

of Meshech and Tubal, and prophesy against him ³ and say, Thus says the Lord GOD: Behold, I am against you, O Gog, chief prince of Meshech and Tubal. ⁴ And I will turn you about and put hooks into your jaws, and I will bring you out, and all your army, horses and horsemen, all of them clothed in full armor, a great host, all of them with buckler and shield, wielding swords. ⁵ Persia, Cush, and Put are with them, all of them with shield and helmet; ⁶ Gomer and all his hordes; Beth-togarmah from the uttermost parts of the north with all his hordes—many peoples are with you." (Ezek 38:1–6)

This confusion stems from the mistranslation of the Jewish word *Rosh* by a few Bible translations such as Young's Literal Translation:

And there is a word of Jehovah unto me, saying: ² "Son of man, set thy face unto Gog, of the land of Magog, prince of Rosh, Meshech, and Tubal, and prophesy concerning him, ³ and thou hast said: Thus, saith the Lord Jehovah: Lo, I [am] against thee, O Gog, Prince of Rosh, Meshech, and Tubal." (Ezek 38:1–3 YLT).

This has led many scholars to suggest that Rosh is a reference to Russia. This is due to the fact that whereas other countries mentioned in the prophecy were existing at the time the prophecy was given, there was no country known as Rosh in existence then. The table of nations in *Holman Bible Atlas* shows an ancient map of some parts of the Near East, listing all the countries in Ezek 38, with no mention of Rosh.[2] Thus, these biblical scholars are forced to rashly conclude that Rosh must be referring to a future country, and the closest country that matches this is Russia!

However, *Rosh* is a Hebrew word that could mean chief, head, beginning, etc, as rightly translated by many Bible versions, including the English Standard Version, King James Version, New Living Translation, etc. (see box 7.1).

Interestingly, most of the countries directly mentioned in the prophecy (Magog Meshech, Tubal, Gomer, Beth-togarmah) are all part of contemporary Turkey. Others not in Turkey are easily identifiable in the contemporary world: Persia (Iran), Cush (Sudan, Ethiopia, and perhaps some parts of Egypt), and Put (Libya).[3]

Thus, putting this back into context, the contemporary superpower may play some indirect role in the end-time events; however, the center

---

2. Brisco, *Holman Bible Atlas*, 36, plate 16.
3. Brisco, *Holman Bible Atlas*, 36, plate 16.

stage according to biblical prophecies will be the Near East, with Turkey, Iran, and Israel being the key players of the event.

The superpowers may also engage in other wars before or during these events as part of the second seal wars (nations against nations, kingdoms against kingdoms—see §3.5) that may orchestrate or usher in the greater wars that will engulf the Near East. Furthermore, during the reign of the antichrist, most of these nations will either support the antichrist or be subjugated by him. Recall that before the battle of Armageddon, the dragon, antichrist, and the false prophet gather all the nations to fight against Christ and his army, under the command of the antichrist.

Box 7.1. Selected Translations of Ezek 38:2–3

And there is a word of Jehovah unto me, saying: ² 'Son of man, set thy face unto Gog, of the land of Magog, prince of Rosh, Meshech, and Tubal, and prophesy concerning him, ³ and thou hast said: Thus, saith the Lord Jehovah: Lo, I [am] against thee, O Gog, Prince of Rosh, Meshech, and Tubal. (YLT)
Here is another message to me from the Lord: 2–3 "Son of dust, face northward toward the land of Magog and prophesy against Gog king of Meshech and Tubal. Tell him that the Lord God says: 'I am against you, Gog. (LB)
And the word of the LORD came unto me, saying,   ² Son of man, set thy face against Gog, the land of Magog, the chief prince of Meshech and Tubal, and prophesy against him,   ³ And say, Thus saith the Lord GOD; Behold, I am against thee, O Gog, the chief prince of Meshech and Tubal. (AV)
This is another message that came to me from the LORD: ² "Son of man, turn and face Gog of the land of Magog, the prince who rules over the nations of Meshech and Tubal, and prophesy against him. ³ Give him this message from the Sovereign LORD: Gog, I am your enemy! (NLT)
The word of the LORD came to me: ² "Son of man, set your face toward Gog, of the land of Magog, the chief prince of Meshech and Tubal, and prophesy against him ³ and say, Thus says the Lord GOD: Behold, I am against you, O Gog, chief prince of Meshech and Tubal. (RSV Catholic ed)

7.9. WHAT-IF SCENARIO: HAS THE FIRST SEAL BEEN BROKEN?

What if the first seal has already been opened and the white horse rider (§3.4) is already riding across the earth? There is a possibility that the world may have missed the entry of the white horse rider onto the stage. While the COVID-19 pandemic was raging across the world, bringing country after country to its knees, there were various speculations about it, as the world grappled to understand its origin, causes, and worldly and spiritual implications. A less obvious hypothesis believed that COVID-19 might be an event linked to the white horse rider.[4] This hypothesis was largely based on three key elements: white horse, bow, and crown. White may signify an apparent innocuous event but potent enough to cripple countries/world (conquering) like any war does. COVID-19 also provided an opportunity that many governments around the world used to gain a lot of powers. The massive powers acquired by the various governments and already enshrined in the laws of the countries could easily be transferred to an individual or the antichrist. The Global Pandemic Accord being championed by the WHO could be a vehicle through which these powers acquired by the various countries could be pulled into one organization/individual. The World Health Assembly is championing a global process to draft and negotiate a convention, agreement, or other international instrument under the constitution of the World Health Organization to strengthen pandemic prevention, preparedness. and response.[5] If the accord/treaty is adopted and ratified, it can be used to force governments to impose certain domestic rules and restrictions such as domestic lockdowns, travel bans, etc.[6] If this scenario of the white horse is correct, it may be that the antichrist is already in place and quietly gaining power around the world.

While this hypothesis sounded quite outlandish at the time, one of the supporting arguments hinged it on a future event—war! According to that, if the pandemic is followed by war, it might be an indication that the second seal, which ushers in the red horse rider, may have been opened. The red horse is characterized by wars (§3.5). It is uncanny how Russian-Ukrainian war commenced as the COVID pandemic was receding across the globe. If this war continues or more countries join (leading to a world war), or other wars erupt between other countries, it would be a time to carefully watch, as this might show that we are living in the end-time period. This would definitely be confirmed if a major war breaks out in the Middle East with Iran charging against neighbouring countries. The conflict between Iran and a confederation led by Turkey would be the clincher (§3.5.3). This would mean that the black horse rider will follow next—devastating famine, economic crisis that will lead to extreme global inflation. Already, the conflict between Russia and Ukraine is affecting global energy and food supply. Many countries are facing increasing difficult economic situations,

4. Harding, "Could Coronavirus."
5. WHO, "World Health Assembly."
6. Qaisrani, "Global Pandemic Accord."

and serious food shortages are projected. Only recently, the governor of the Bank of England, Andrew Bailey, painted a bleak picture of the global economy for the coming months. The governor told MPs on the UK Treasury Select Committee that he was helpless in the face of skyrocketing inflation rates in the country. He warned of apocalyptic global food shortage. Interestingly, he was quoted to have said that he has "run out of horsemen" (a reference to the four horsemen of Revelation), when counting the shocks facing Britain, with increasing energy and food costs.[7] The choice of words by the governor, bringing in "apocalyptic" and the "horsemen" might be a pointer or cue to say we might be in this long-predicted period.

Following the black would be the pale horse—pestilence. If this scenario is correct, it means that either the COVID pandemic will be raging via a variant of the virus or another pandemic that will be deadlier than COVID-19. When this happens, people should get ready for the emergence of the antichrist on the global stage. Indeed, this is a time that we all need to watch and pray as Christ admonished.

A crucial point to note is that the four horsemen, although appearing sequentially, might at some point work together (their actions intersecting with those following them). Revelation did not record any of the horsemen being withdrawn from the scene once they have been unleashed. This implies that that the events will continue regardless of others subsequently joining them. This is captured after the rider of pale horse entered the stage:

> I looked, and there before me was a pale horse! Its rider was named Death, and Hades was following close behind him. They were given power over a fourth of the earth to kill by sword, famine and plague, and by the wild beasts of the earth. (Rev 6:8 NIV)

The horsemen were given power to kill one quarter of the global population with sword (war), famine (hunger) and plague (pandemic).

7.10. PARABLE OF THE TEN VIRGINS—THE PHILADELPHIA VS THE LAODICEAN CHURCH

> Then the kingdom of heaven will be like ten virgins who took their lamps and went to meet the bridegroom. ² Five of them were foolish, and five were wise. ³ For when the foolish took their lamps, they took no oil with them, ⁴ but the wise took flasks of oil with their lamps. ⁵ As the bridegroom was delayed, they all became drowsy and slept. ⁶ But at midnight there was a

---

7. Wallace, "Bank of England Warns."

> cry, "Here is the bridegroom! Come out to meet him." ⁷ Then all those virgins rose and trimmed their lamps. ⁸ And the foolish said to the wise, "Give us some of your oil, for our lamps are going out." ⁹ But the wise answered, saying, "Since there will not be enough for us and for you, go rather to the dealers and buy for yourselves." ¹⁰ And while they were going to buy, the bridegroom came, and those who were ready went in with him to the marriage feast, and the door was shut. ¹¹ Afterward the other virgins came also, saying, "Lord, lord, open to us." ¹² But he answered, "Truly, I say to you, I do not know you." ¹³ Watch therefore, for you know neither the day nor the hour. (Matt 25:1–13)

The parable of the ten virgins tends to point towards two groups of Christians that will be on earth just before the return of Christ. Both groups of people are Christians (virgins); however, one group (the wise ones) are well prepared for any eventuality that could happen during the waiting period, while the others (foolish ones) will not be entirely tuned to the events of the time and hence not fully prepared for the eventuality. *Hence, when the wise ones who assiduously worked for the kingdom of God are taken to a place of preservation, the rest will have to face the wrath of the dragon and antichrist:*

> Because you have kept my word about patient endurance, I will keep you from the hour of trial that is coming on the whole world, to try those who dwell on the earth. (Rev 3:10)

> Behold, I have set before you an open door, which no one is able to shut. (Rev 3:8)

The five wise virgins may also represent the group of Christians who prepared for any eventuality (long wait for the bridegroom) that may arise during the end-time, including facing the hardship of the great tribulation, while the five foolish virgins may represent those Christians who believed in a rapture that would take them out of the world before the troubles start. Hence, when the trouble starts, they are unable to withstand till the coming of the bridegroom.

7.11. CONCLUSION

Jesus is coming back to the earth to set up his everlasting kingdom.

For this to happen, Satan and his cohorts who are holding sway in this world must be crushed. After Satan and the antichrist have been defeated, Christ will set up his kingdom on earth that will initially last for one thousand years. After this, there will be another war, the final war that will lead to the ultimate defeat of Satan and his followers, who will be thrown into the lake of fire. Then the present earth and heaven will come to an end, and a new earth and new heaven will emerge.

There is an appointed time of great distress that is coming upon the earth. The day and hour no one knows, except our heavenly Father. However, there are certain indicators that people who are alert and watching may use to gain some insights on when the aforementioned events will commence.

This book has explored some of those indicators and signs in detail to aid many to understand these and to reduce unnecessary anxiety, especially among Christians.

We should all prepare to face this period of great tribulation. But if, out of the mercy of God, some of us are preserved or allowed to escape some of the difficulties of the time, that would be great. However, the best approach in life is to prepare for the worst and accept the good turn.

For unbelievers, there is still time to come to Christ; and for believers, this is time to intensify our efforts in doing things that are pleasing to God:

> "Even now," declares the LORD, "return to me with all your heart,
> with fasting and weeping and mourning."
> [13] Rend your heart and not your garments. Return to the LORD your God, for he is gracious and compassionate, slow to anger and abounding in love, and he relents from sending calamity.
> (Joel 2:12–13)

With regards to rapture conventionally understood as the taking out from the earth transformed humans (dead and living) to heaven in a twinkle of an eye, in order to escape the great tribulation, it has been incredibly difficult for me to find a verse in the Bible that supports this. So, this theory could have been based on misinterpretation of Bible verses. Every individual must endeavor to work this (rapture or no rapture) out for himself/herself. Importantly, remember Christ's prime warning for the end-time period:

> See that no one leads you astray. (Matt 24:4)

Also, while reading Revelation, it is important to put into consideration that there may have been some hyperbole used in the signs and writings, especially when some events reported as "all nations," "the whole world," "all the people," etc. are mentioned.

Bibliography

Arendzen, J. P. "Hypsistarians." Catholic Answers; orig. from *Catholic Encylopedia*, 1907–1912. https://www.catholic.com/encyclopedia/hypsistarians.

Brisco, Thomas V. *Holman Bible Atlas*. Nashville: Broadman & Holman, 1998.

Fairchild, Mary. "The Meaning of the 7 Churches of Revelation." Learn Religions, updated Dec. 9, 2019. https://www.learnreligions.com/churches-of-revelation-4145039.

Gorvett, Jonathan. "Turkey's Vision of a Brave, New Ottoman Empire." *Asia Times*, June 17, 2020. https://asiatimes.com/2020/06/turkeys-vision-of-a-brave-new-ottoman-empire/.

Hamed, Adham. "How Will Russia, China and Iran's Alliance Pose a Threat to the US?" *Al-Estiklal*, Mar. 2022. https://www.alestiklal.net/en/view/12004/how-will-russia-china-and-irans-alliance-pose-a-threat-to-the-us.

Harding, Luke. "Could Coronavirus Be the First Horseman of the Apocalypse?" YouTube, 2021. https://www.youtube.com/watch?v=DBsNlnNcR7Q.

Jeremiah, David. "Seven Churches of Revelation Bible Study." David Jeremiah, n.d. https://davidjeremiah.blog/seven-churches-of-revelation-bible-study/.

Lederer, Edith M. "Cyprus' Top Diplomat: Turkey Is Creating New Ottoman Empire." *ABC News*, Sept. 29, 2021. https://abcnews.go.com/US/wireStory/cyprus-top-diplomat-turkey-creating-ottoman-empire-80302961.

Mackie, Tim. "The Significance of Seven." BibleProject, Oct. 21, 2019. Podcast. https://bibleproject.com/podcast/significance-7/#:~:text=Seven%20was%20symbolic%20in%20ancient,seven%E2%80%9D%20patterns%20in%20the%20Bible.

Melton, J. Gordon. "New Age Movement." *Encyclopedia Britannica*, Apr. 7, 2016. https://www.britannica.com/topic/New-Age-movement.

Qaisrani, Anjum. "Global Pandemic Accord Set to Extend WHO Powers during Pandemic." *Analyst*, May 17, 2022. https://www.analystnews.com/society/%ef%bf%bcglobal-pandemic-accord-set-to-extend-who-powers-during-outbreak/.

Rivera, Laura S. "7 Churches of Revelation Modern Map." Maps for You Free, Jan. 2016. https://mapsforyoufree.blogspot.com/2016/01/7-churches-of-revelation-modern-map.html.

Theopedia. "Irenaeus." Theopedia, n.d. https://www.theopedia.com/irenaeus.

———. "Nicolaitans." Theopedia, n.d. https://www.theopedia.com/nicolaitans.

Ugfacts. "Where to Buy Wormwood in South Africa 2022–2023." Ugfacts, Apr. 4, 2022. https://ugfacts.net/za/where-to-buy-wormwood-in-south-africa/.

Verrett, Bethany. "What Is the Significance of the Seven Churches in Revelation?" Bible Study Tools, Aug. 11, 2020. https://www.biblestudytools.com/bible-study/topical-studies/what-is-the-significance-of-the-seven-churches-in-revelation.html.

Wallace, Tim. "Bank of England Warns of 'Apocalyptic' Global Food Shortage." *Telegraph*, May 16, 2022. https://www.telegraph.co.uk/business/2022/05/16/bank-england-warns-apocalyptic-global-food-shortage/.

WHO. "World Health Assembly Agrees to Launch Process to Develop Historic Global Accord on Pandemic Prevention, Preparedness and Response." World Health Organization, Dec. 1, 2021. https://www.who.int/news/item/01-12-2021-world-health-assembly-agrees-to-launch-process-to-develop-historic-global-accord-on-pandemic-prevention-preparedness-and-response.

www.ingramcontent.com/pod-product-compliance
Lightning Source LLC
Chambersburg PA
CBHW051057160426
43193CB00010B/1224